STRONG MEN SERIES STUDY GUIDE

THE TRAIL'S END

BOOK 5: FINISHING STRONG

JIM RAMOS

COPYRIGHT

© 2021 Jim Ramos

All rights reserved. No part of this publication may be reproduced, distributed, or transmitted in any form or by any means, including photocopying, recording, or other electronic or mechanical methods, without the prior written permission of the publisher, except in the case of brief quotations embodied in critical reviews and certain other noncommercial uses permitted by copyright law. For permission requests, contact Five Stones Press or Jim Ramos

Publisher: Five Stones Press, Dallas, Texas

For quantity sales, textbooks, and orders by trade bookstores or wholesalers contact Five Stones Press at connect@fivestonespeople.com

Five Stones Press is owned and operated by Five Stones Church, a nonprofit 501c3 religious organization. Press name and logo are trademarked. Contact publisher for use.

Jim Ramos's website is www.meninthearena.org - Men in the Arena can bring speakers to your organization to teach the principles covered in this book.

All chapter entries are listed in order according to where they appear in Scripture. Unless noted the entries are from the New American Standard Bible (NASB).

All other Scripture quotations are taken from the New American Standard Bible, ©1960, 1962, 1963, 1968, 1971, 1972, 1973, 1975, 1977, 1995 by The Lockman Foundation. Used by permission. Additional versions used are:
KJV—King James Version. Authorized King James Version.
NIV—Scripture taken from the Holy Bible, New International Version®. Copyright © 1973, 1978, 1984 by International Bible Society. Used by permission of Zondervan Publishing House. All rights reserved.

Printed in the United States of America

DEDICATION

The Trail's End is dedicated to my Mom. I'm a mommy's boy. I admit it. My mother and I have had a special relationship all my life. From the way she tells my hilarious birth story every December to her tactful way of dealing with difficult people, she is the epitome of grace and peace.

In 2012, she exhibited a new strength when my Stepdad tragically ended his life. It was then that Mom was forced to navigate through the murky waters of a good man who—for whatever reason—finished wrong. She, like so many women, has championed the struggle for purpose when life left her with questions that had no answers.

I'm a blessed to have such a wonderful woman to call my Mom. I will viciously protect her from anything that threatens her in any way. She is my hero. I love you Mom.

Freshman Formal 1981   Wedding Day 1992   James' College Graduation 2016

TEAM CAPTAIN RESOURCES

You've received The Strong Men Series at a conference, from our website, your pastor, or possibly a friend. Now what? If you're holding this book, then you are a magnum enough man to figure it out on your own. This book is dangerous and has the power to change lives because within its pages are reference after reference from the Book of books.

You may still have some questions; we know this. We've provided several resources to help you on your journey to transform the lives of men and those they love, because when a man gets it—everyone wins.

First, check out our website (www.meninthearena.org). There you will find tons of great resources designed to inspire and equip you towards your best version.

Second, join thousands of men from around the world on our exciting Men in the Arena closed Facebook forum for men. Engage with men every day as they dialogue about what a man is and does. Do you need more help? We have a team of Arena Coaches ready to help you!

Third, subscribe to our wildly popular Men in the Arena Podcast. The Men in the Arena Podcast targets men living in the "Stress Bubble of Life" who are hardworking, loving one wife, raising godly children, and serving in their community.

Fourth, check out the QR Code before each meeting that links to an introductory video. Each video will help guide you to the best meeting possible.

SEND US A PICTURE OF YOUR TEAM

SEND US A PICTURE OF YOUR TEAM AND YOUR HERO STORY

We have no way of knowing who our resources are impacting, but we'd love to celebrate with you. Send us a picture of your team. We'll post it on social media and in our monthly newsletter if the photo is high quality and we have space.

Also, send us your stories of transformation that we call Hero Stories. God is the famous one, but He has chosen you to be the hero for your family. When a man gets it—everyone wins. If we happen to share your story, we will shoot you some swag to say, "Thanks!"

When you send the team picture, let us know where you're from (city, state, and/or country), who the leaders are, and where you meet (coffee shop, living room, church, etc.). Thank you for partnering with us.

INTRODUCTION

Well done, good and faithful servant! You have been faithful with a few things; I will put you in charge of many things. Come and share your master's happiness!
Matthew 25:21

Keep the ice chest cold and filled. It's often a long walk back to the truck and even a longer drive home. Of all my hunting memories, I vividly recall the special care Dad took to fill the ice chest with cold drinks. It was a small reward for a hard day in the California heat. Knowing an ice-cold soda was waiting at the Jeep kept me pressing on. Nothing tastes better than your favorite chilled beverage after sucking lukewarm water from a World War II canteen.

As a young teenager in the 80's my drink of choice was an ice-cold Mountain Dew. Oh, that cold lemon lime taste—out of an ice chest and down my throat! I took their 80's slogan to heart at the end of a hard day, "Give me a Dew!"

Like the end of the trail those memories spent with Dad and my brother, Tom, are days long gone. At some point, everything ends—even life. As much as we'd like to ignore it we all face the end of the trail, some sooner than others. The author of Hebrews wisely penned, "It is appointed for men to die once and after this comes judgment" (Hebrews 9:27 NASB).

Every man finishes life.

But not all finish strong.

Oh, to hear those refreshing words, "Well done" (Matthew 25:21) after a lifetime of clawing, scratching, and fighting to push back the darkness for God's glory. How I long to hear those words from my Master—my King!

Don't buy society's lie to work hard, retire, and coast to the end of life's trail. This couldn't be further from Biblical truth. Too many men have put their face to the grindstone only to be forgotten on their tombstone. Cherish your life. You only have one. Enjoy the scenic views on your journey. Live at a pace that allows you to capture the essence of life and finish strong.

I heard a Christian leader of men, Chuck Stecker, passionately admonish older men, "If you've passed the baton, take it back!" In other words, don't stop serving God until He takes the final breath from your fighting lungs. I'd rather burn out in a blaze of glory than rust out by succumbing to life's elements.

If done right a man's greatest years are his final years, when he can enjoy the benefits of wisdom gained over a lifetime ascent up the mountain of God. It's in his twilight that a man's voice echoes most powerfully to the younger generations. Proverbs 17:6 reminds us of the truth that, "Children's children are a crown to the aged, and parents are the pride of their children."

If you've passed the baton, take it back. Finish your life strong. Life is more than the hike out of a scorching canyon and noon. It's about those moments at the truck over an ice-cold drink with someone you love—after that we learn the joy of a life well lived.

There are finishes and there are strong finishes. They are not the same. Sometimes a finish is a wrong finish. A divorce is a wrong finish. A suicide is a wrong finish. Getting fired from your job for reasons you could have avoided is a wrong finish. To live selfishly in retirement, refusing to impact others with your experiences, wisdom, and expertise is a wrong finish.

It may be the most tragic finish of them all.

Commit yourself at all costs to finishing strong.

As Matthew Henry once wrote, "It ought to be the business every day to prepare for the final day."

TABLE OF CONTENTS

THE EXCLAMATION POINT — 10

THE GOOD FIGHT — 22

NO SECRETS — 32

  MEN ON THE ROOF — 42

  COVENANT EYES — 54

  BEFORE THE FALL — 64

FRONT END ALIGNMENT — 74

THE SERIOUS LIFE — 86

REST; A FOUR LETTER WORD — 96

FIGHTING SPIRIT — 106

A WORD FROM THE AUTHOR

Welcome to the multimedia edition of the Strong Men Study Series. In this new edition we've added QR codes at the beginning of each chapter. You can scan the QR codes with your smartphone or tablet to access all team meeting introductory videos.

In these videos we introduce you to the content of each study. These brief presentations are designed to prepare your mind and heart for each team study.

At the end of the book you'll see a page called, "New Team Launch Steps" with QR codes leading up to your Men in the Arena team launch. The videos are a great resource for any man desiring to launch a new team. We emphatically recommend that every man partner with another man, to eventually start his own team. You've got this!

There are many QR readers available for smartphones and tablets. Check your device. It may already have one installed. Thank you so much for championing the cause of Christ on behalf of men because when a man gets it—everyone wins.

Jim Ramos

TEAM MEETING ONE:
THE EXCLAMATION POINT

> *"It's not how you start that matters. It's how you finish."*
> ~ Steve Farrar, *Finishing Strong*

Welcome to the fifth and final book in The Strong Men Series—The Trail's End. Leaning against a bookshelf in my office is a white cardboard box standing about four feet tall. It's a gun box, but not just any gun box. This box held a Remington Model 700 chambered in .270 caliber. I know the gun because I helped Mom pick it out for my stepdad as a Christmas gift.

If you get close enough to the box you'll be able to read the handwriting describing where it was found: "Found next to the body." On December 21, 2012, my Stepfather used the gun to take his own life; the gun was returned in this box. Why he took his own life, we'll never know. He was a good man. He was a wonderful stepfather.

He worked hard. He owned a beautiful home. He was healthy. For more than three decades he loved Mom. He was loved at the golf course where he worked part time as a Marshal. In fact, everyone loved him. Everything seemed fine. His death was shocking. His loved ones are left with unanswered questions.

Whenever I hear his name or see that gun box I remember his tragic end. The box serves as a reminder that my loved ones are counting on me to finish strong. Mom asked me to keep the box and use it to help men avoid wrong finishes—finishes that leave more questions than answers.

Some men live strong for a season but finish wrong. Life's a tough journey but one that can be finished well. These ten team meetings and fifty daily readings are designed to inspire men to finish everyday with an exclamation point and not a question mark.

Welcome to The Trail's End.

TEAM MEETING AT A GLANCE
- Opening Prayer, Weekly Announcements
- Personal and Victory Stories
- Each man will share his story — one man per week until all men have shared.
- After all men have shared their personal story, allow time each week for them to share victory stories.
- Weekly Study Closing Prayer
- Closing Prayer

> *"Starts are not nearly as important as finishes."*
> ~Duane Emry

Each of you us have a chance to answer. How is finishing different from finishing strong? Can you share a personal example of a wrong finish instead of a strong one?

"The end of a matter is better than its beginning, and patience is better than pride."
Ecclesiastes 7:8

Why do some men finish strong while others finish wrong? What did Jesus say about finishing?
Luke 14:28-30

Finishing strong is a New Testament principle. Wrong finishes are worldly and not in God's plan. Divorce, getting fired from a job (with just cause), suicide, and retirement (from serving God) are products of human depravity—not God. What do the following New Testament passages teach about finishing?
2 Corinthians 8:10-12, Acts 20:24, and 2 Timothy 4:6-8

Live at a pace you can handle. Run a race that you can finish. Generally speaking, you'll be remembered for your ending, not your beginning. You don't have to be the best. You just have to outlast the rest.

> *"Let's put it on the table. If you're not teachable, you don't have a chance in the world of finishing strong. Not a chance."*
> ~Steve Farrar, *Finishing Strong*

What would Jesus say about finishing strong versus finishing wrong? What examples of finishing did Jesus leave for us to imitate?
Luke 12:49-51, John 4:34-35, 5:35-36, 19:28-30, and Hebrews 12:1-3

After this, Jesus, knowing that all things had already been accomplished, to fulfill the Scripture, said, "I am thirsty." A jar full of sour wine was standing there; so they put a sponge full of the sour wine upon a branch of hyssop and brought it up to His mouth. Therefore when Jesus had received the sour wine, He said, "It is finished!" And He bowed His head and gave up His spirit.
John 19:28-30

Take a moment to look up various Bible translations for John 19:30. You can find them if you have them with most Bible applications on your smartphone. Do you notice anything? How are the various translations similar? How are they different?

Neither the Hebrew nor Greek languages use punctuation points. Because of this, Bible translators are compelled to guess where punctuation goes for the English language. Here are some Bible translations that include an exclamation point after Jesus' "It is finished!" statement from the cross: New American Standard (NASB), New Living Translation (NLT), New King James (NKJV), Contemporary English Version (CEV), JB Phillips, and (my favorite) Hawai'i Pidgin (HWP).

> *Wen Jesus wen suck da cheap wine he say,*
> *"Every ting pau awready!"*
> *An he wen bend down his head, an den let go his spirit.*
> John 19:30 (HWP)

Would you put an exclamation point on the end of Jesus' finish on the cross, a period, colon (King James Version), or some other punctuation mark? Which Jesus do you see on the cross? Did He finish with a whine, a whimper, or a war cry? How do these simple punctuation marks make all the difference in how men see Jesus?

> *"Finishing life strong is the simple result of finishing every day strong compounded over a lifetime."*
> ~Men in the Arena

> *"Jesus died with a shout of triumph on his lips. He did not say, 'It is finished,' in weary defeat; He said it as one who shouts for joy because the victory was won."*
> ~William Barclay

The expression ('It is finished!') may be interpreted in various ways: as a cry of relief, because suffering is ending; as a cry of anguish, because his ministry has ended in failure; or as a shout of victory, because the purpose of God has triumphed in his death. The last of these seems to be the author's intent. He makes it the final report of Jesus to the Father, who will now exalt him to glory. The final word says, 'he bowed his head and gave up his spirit' could also be translated 'he laid his head to rest and dismissed his spirit.' Jesus retained consciousness and command of himself till the very end."
~Expositor's Bible Commentary

Men in the Arena's definition of manhood is, "protecting integrity, fighting apathy, pursuing God passionately, leading courageously, and finishing strong." Why do you think the verbs are strategically crafted in the progressive tense (ending with "ing")?

Why is the word "strong" attached to "finishing"?
"(In John 19:30) The verb form of finished means: 'It is finished...and now still is finished'. It's an action whose results or effects go on; an action leaving a condition or state of lasting significance or status."
~The Discovery Bible

Finishing life strong is little more than finishing every day strong compounded over a lifetime. What do the following verses teach about being a daily finisher?
Matthew 6:11, Luke 9:23, and 1 Thessalonians 4:11-12

How Jesus finished is everything. The exclamation point is everything. Men, the problem is that too many of us don't live for the exclamation point. We leave this world with questions, commas, or dashes. We retire and fade away. We quit shy of the finish line. We end short of the victory chant—not Jesus. He pushed through the pain to the exclamation point. How he finished is everything. How you finish is everything too.

> *"You don't have to be the best. You just have to outlast the rest."*
> ~The Great Hunt for God

Matthew Henry (1662-1714) was a Nonconformist minister and author from England. What wisdom can we gain from his quote (below)? How do the following verses help us see the end of our life? Matthew 25:21-23 and Luke 17:10

Put an exclamation point at the end of each and every day of your life. What you do today, compounded over time is more important than you can ever imagine? How will you finish today? How will you finish your life?
Matthew 10:21-23, 24:12-14, Ephesians 6:13-15, Philippians 1:6, 1:27, and 1 Corinthians 16:13

What is your greatest temptation to not finish each day strong after you get home from work. How do you overcome weakness to finish each day strong?
Proverbs 23:4, Galatians 6:9, 2 Thessalonians 3:12-14, and Hebrews 12:3

You may be a wrong finisher if you have a history of making excuses about quitting. You verbally support quitters and quitting. You live a transient life. You have a track record of wrong finishes. Your community roots are shallow. You're a jack-of-all-trades, but master of none. You refuse to volunteer in serving others according to your abilities.

You're indifferent about training up the next generation. You're disconnected from your children and grandchildren. You retired from serving God when you retired from your career. You've passed the baton to the next generation and left the race. You wordsmith "quitting" to sound better than it is. If more than two of these describe you, it's time to stand up, put an exclamation point on today, and fix the problem you've created.

Break into groups of three or four.

What part of your day needs an exclamation point? Where are you failing to finish strong in your daily life?

Take a moment today and pray for each other.

> *"It ought to be the business every day to prepare for the final day."*
> ~Matthew Henry

STUDY NOTES

For the next five days, read the following entries from our **The Field Guide: A Bathroom Book for Men.**

We hope they challenge and encourage you to get in the great Arena for God. See you on the Arena Floor!

BARNABAS

He was a good man, full of the Holy Spirit and faith, and a great number of people were brought to the Lord.
Acts 11:24

In The Seven Habits of Highly Effective People Steven Covey writes, "See the end at the beginning." Author Henry Cloud agrees in Nine Things You Simply Must Do by admonishing readers to, "Play the movie."

Several years ago, I attempted to see the end by writing my obituary. As difficult as this was, it allowed me to put my legacy on paper. I still weep every time I read it. As a family leader, a man must see the end of The Stress Bubble at the beginning. Play it out. What does it look like? Write your obituary.

Or, for those who really want challenge write your epitaph. What short phrase would your loved ones inscribe on your tombstone? In Acts 11:24 we get a shot at Barnabas' epitaph; "He was a good man." Barnabas was an encourager. He was the first disciple in Jerusalem to take a risk and reach out to Paul (Acts 9:27). He was comfortable sitting second chair to the great Apostle Paul.

But he wasn't less than Paul. In fact, when ministering in Lystra the people believed the Greek gods had manifested—giving Paul the title of Hermes—because he was the main speaker. But to Barnabas they gave the higher title of Zeus.

Zeus?

Yes, Barnabas was given the highest title of all Greek gods (Acts 14:12-13).

How will you be remembered? Does the life you're living reflect how you want to be remembered? If not, change your life. Change your epitaph while you're living.

Are you upright or upside down?

PLAY THE MOVIE

"It ought to be the business every day to prepare for the final day."
Matthew Henry

Play the movie of your life. If you're to continue the path you're on, where will you be a the end of your life? How are your relationships? How's your marriage doing? How are your children? Are you serving the Lord? Are you giving to causes that you love?

Examine your habits and ask, "If I continue on the road I've mapped for today, what will life look like in the future?" Many marriages would be redeemed and children saved if men would only "play the movie" before choosing to experience it in living color.

God has set eternity in our hearts (Ecclesiastes 3:11). When man was made in the Imago Dei—image of God—he was given a wonderful gift that separates him from every living thing. He was given a soul. With a soul man can discern moral absolutes, determine his eternal destiny, and decide on more than his primary needs of survival.

In the parable of the talents found in Matthew 25:14-28 we read about two men who knew their master's heart and invested according to their abilities. The third man, however, buried his talent in the sand. Instead of hearing "Well done my good and faithful servant," he was condemned with,

"You wicked, lazy servant!"

What will it be? You choose.

Will you play the movie of your life? Will you see the end of your life now? Will you prepare every day as if it were your last?

Live today to the fullest (John 10:10). Start now.

Make it your business today to prepare for your final day.

EXPERIENCE AND WISDOM

You have made my days a mere handbreadth; the span of my years is as nothing before you. Each man's life is but a breath.
Psalm 39: 5

At the end of a father-and-son retreat I came home with a twisted knee, pulled oblique, and strained hamstring from playing whiffle ball and basketball with young men in my youth group.

Rounding the corner on the halftime of life is apparent these days. Age reveals the ceiling of our lives. We aren't invincible. We feel the age in our bones. Our dreams get hidden behind the walls of reality. The fire burns down to coals. The options become fewer.

How do we run the second half of life with more effectiveness? Where do we learn to work smarter not harder in the second half? How can we adjust our dreams of a hungry soul but aging body?

There's a real tension between spiritually maturing and physically diminishing. Listen to Paul's tension with growing older in 2 Corinthians 4:16, "Therefore we do not lose heart. Though outwardly we are wasting away, yet inwardly we are being renewed day by day."

After halftime, adjusting our fire isn't as simple as in our younger days. We need to navigate the second half wisely. We need to know God's will more than ever. Especially because the older we get the more people depend on our leadership. Lapses in judgment have greater consequence and effect more lives the older we become.

But all is not lost.

With age comes wisdom.

Ah, wisdom.

With age comes a deeper sense of God's faithfulness. We can exhale and trust in God's plan in the second half.

Just as energy and strength were the pillars in the first half of life, experience and wisdom are even greater weapons in the second half. Use them.

DESTROYER

The thief comes to steal, kill and destroy...
John 10:10a

The first album I purchased as a young boy was Destroyer by the rock band Kiss. The awesome cover, curious face paint of band members, and the hammering rock and roll sounds of their music enthralled me. Destroyer was Kiss' fourth album, released in 1976, and was their first to achieve platinum.

I can still draw each of the four members' face paint, and recall the words to songs such as, Detroit Rock City, God of Thunder and, of course, Beth. Besides the rock band, Destroyer also makes us consider Satan. John 10:10a plainly warns, "The thief (Satan) comes to steal, kill and destroy."

In John 10:10b Jesus continues, "I have come that they may have life, and have it to the full." I've often reflected on what Jesus meant about, "steal, kill, and destroy" and have concluded that this is a progression of Satan's destructive plan for our lives.

Satan wants to steal from God's children. He want to steal a young man's virginity. He wants to rob you of the first love of your faith, joy, and whatever else he can rip from your life.

After stealing, his next desire is to kill you. He wants to kill your faith, marriage, relationships, commitment to the local church—ultimately you! Yes, he wants you dead and buried and will stop at nothing to see you in the dirt.

Ultimately, however, he wants to destroy you. He wants your lineage— your spiritual family tree—to die with you. If he can kill the faith of your children then he's succeeded in destroying your eternal legacy.

Does this need an explanation? Finishing strong means more than just finishing. It means taking others with us to heaven—legacy.

Fight for your lasting legacy. Your enemy is.

SHAVING PARTNERS

The heart is deceitful above all things and beyond cure. Who can understand it? "I the Lord search the heart and examine the mind, to reward a man according to his conduct, according to what his deeds deserve."
Jeremiah 17:9-10

I listened to financial expert Dave Ramsey talk about money management. He grimaced while telling his audience that getting one's money in order is a difficult task. Then, relaxing his face and grinning, Ramsey moved across the stage poised with the knowledge of what was coming next, "Managing your money is the easiest thing in the world!"

He explained that if it were not for the man he shaved with, he would be rich and skinny! According to James 1:13-14 a man's biggest enemy is indeed the man in the mirror. "When tempted, no one should say, 'God is tempting me.' For God cannot be tempted by evil, nor does he tempt anyone; but each one is tempted when, by his own evil desire, he is dragged away and enticed."

A boy surrenders his heart to the man in the mirror. He gives into the temptation of his youth. He struggles against that guy staring back at him. The greatest challenge for the man in the mirror is his struggle against sin. It's the battle to align his private life with his public image. We all know men who say the right things, but act differently.

Live without secrets.

Bring your darkness into the light. Actions speak loud, but not loud enough. God searches the hearts of men and desires to align our actions to His heart. Does your life align with your heart?

TEAM MEETING TWO: THE GOOD FIGHT

> *"A quitter never wins but a winner never quits."*
> ~Coaches Office Window

What did you take away from last week's study and daily readings? What are you still processing? What challenged your current paradigm? What inspired you to grow as a man?

How often do you see bad fights on the news? If you've been in one you know how futile it can be. What are some characteristics of a bad fight? Why do people engage in this kind of behavior? How can you protect yourself from fighting a bad fight?

For I am already being poured out like a drink offering, and the time for my departure is near. I have fought the good fight, I have finished the race, I have kept the faith. Now there is in store for me the crown of righteousness, which the Lord, the righteous Judge, will award to me on that day—and not only to me, but also to all who have longed for his appearing.
2 Timothy 4:6-8

Read 2 Timothy 4:1-8 above. What good fight is Paul talking about? What did Paul mean in 2 Timothy 4:7 by, "I have fought the good fight"?
1 Corinthians 9:26-27, 1 Timothy 1:18-20, 6:11-14, and Luke 14:28-32

Choose your battles wisely. Too many men waste their lives fighting a bad fight. Before you fight make sure you've counted the cost and considered whether the fight you're about to embark on is good, bad, or ugly.

What kind of finish is Paul talking about in 2 Timothy 4:7 by, "I have finished the race"? What is your recipe for finishing life strong? What advice would you give a younger man?
Ecclesiastes 7:8-10, John 19:30, Hebrews 12:1-3, and
1 Corinthians 9:24-27

22

TEAM MEETING AT A GLANCE

- Opening Prayer, Weekly Announcements
- Personal and Victory Stories
- Each man will share his story — one man per week until all men have shared.
- After all men have shared their personal story, allow time each week for them to share victory stories.
- Weekly Study Closing Prayer
- Closing Prayer

> *"If a man does not finish each day strong he ends it weak, but he must finish more days strong than weak. Weak days compounded equal a weak life."*
> ~The Great Hunt for God

The man who finishes well is nothing more than the man who finishes each day strong, compounded over a lifetime. What you do from 6:00-9:00 each night is more important than you can ever imagine.

It's our daily job as spiritual leaders to see the "end" in endurance. See the "severe" in persevere. What did Paul mean in Colossians 4:17 when he spoke to Archippus?
Romans 5:1-5, 2 Corinthians 11:22-29, 1 Timothy 4:15-16, 2 Timothy 4:4-5, Hebrews 12:7-8, and James 1:2-4, 12

When Paul told Archippus to "fulfill the ministry you have received from the Lord," he used the present infinitive form of the verb "fulfill." This was a command to "fulfill" his ministry consistently or repeatedly over time—as a continuous process or habit. Essentially, Paul admonished Archippus to finish his ministry each and every day.

What kind of faith is Paul talking about in 2 Timothy 4:7 by, "I have kept the faith"? How do we ensure that our faith won't shift or veer off course over time? How do we guard against those things that threaten to pull us off course?
Deuteronomy 6:4-9, Psalm 119:9-16, Matthew 7:24-27, Ephesians 6:10-17, 2 Timothy 3:10-17, 4:1-5, and Hebrews 4:12-13

Let's review 2 Timothy 4:6-8, "I have fought the good fight, I have finished the race, I have kept the faith." At the end of his life, Paul mentioned three components—his good fight, completed race, and enduring faith. Is two out of three good enough to finish strong?

> *"It's the job that's never started that takes the longest to finish."*
> ~J.R.R. Tolkien

Here's another story of a strong a finisher. This man had every reason to quit and walk away. He had the equivalent of vertical cross-eyes. He was colorblind. He had corns on his feet so he could barely wear shoes. He had thin skin, which made him cold constantly and he almost always wore a jacket. He was recognized as the ugliest man to ever hold a high political office. Here is his brief resume.

- Age 22: His business failed
- Age 23: He was defeated for Legislature
- Age 24: He had another failed business venture
- Age 25: He was elected to the Legislature
- Age 26: His sweetheart died
- Age 27: He had a nervous breakdown
- Age 29: He was defeated for House speaker
- Age 31: He was defeated for Elector
- Age 34: He was defeated for Congress
- Age 37: He was elected to Congress
- Age 39: He was defeated for Congress
- Age 46: He was defeated for Senate
- Age 47: He was defeated for VP of the USA
- Age 49: He was defeated for Senate
- Age 51: He was elected as the 16th President of the USA

He is Abraham Lincoln.

Break into groups of three or four.

What spoke to you the most today? How can we pray for you?

Take a moment today and pray for each other.

> *"I'd made it this far and refused to give up because all my life I had always finished the race."*
> ~Louis Zamperini

STUDY NOTES

_____
_____
_____
_____
_____
_____
_____
_____
_____
_____
_____
_____
_____
_____

For the next five days, read the following entries from our **The Field Guide: A Bathroom Book for Men.**

We hope they challenge and encourage you to get in the great Arena for God. See you on the Arena Floor!

EXCLAMATION

When he had received the drink, Jesus said, "It is finished."
With that, he bowed his head and gave up his spirit.
John 19:30

Finishing is more than ending. To finish strong is to finish with integrity and determination. But the temptation is to finish weak just to complete a task. We cheat on our last repetition at the gym. We leave work ten minutes early. We fall asleep on the couch after a long day at work. We retire and put life on cruise control.

But men finish strong not wrong.

Jesus is our example of finishing strong. There's Jesus on the cross. He's beaten. He's bleeding. He's nearly unrecognizable. He's at his breaking point moments before death. Crucifixion was a horrible death by asphyxiation.

In his final moments Jesus struggles to take his final breath. He pushes down on the nail in his feet, driving his raw back along the splintered wood, just high enough for one last gasp of air, and in his final act on earth moans, "It…is…finished."

The New International Version ends there. What a bummer. But the New American Standard adds something vital to our study—an exclamation point.

Jesus didn't say he was finished in a soft and weak voice. He shouted it. He screamed it. It was a victory cry, "It is finished!"

He went Braveheart on that thing. "Freedom!"

Jesus wanted all of eternity to know he had finished strong in the task his Father gave him to do (John 5:36).

He finished strong. He finished with a shout of triumph.

He finished like the model of manhood he is.

He finished with an exclamation point.

THE SPORT OF SIN

Doing wickedness is like sport to a fool, and so is wisdom to a man of understanding.
Proverbs 10:23

A young man once asked, "What's your number, Jim?"

Not understanding his question I asked, "What, like a sleep number bed?"

"No," he replied, "How many women have you slept with?"

Choose your words wisely, I thought. "One!" I said. "Since following Christ I have been true to my wife. That's the only number that matters."

Sin was still a sport to this young man. To him, like so many other young men, bedding women was a game—another notch in the belt. He's finding "pleasure in evil conduct" (NIV).

Before Christ I looked for opportunities to brag about sin. Sin was a game. As an adult follower of Jesus, I am ashamed of it—building guardrails to protect me from the sins I celebrated as a young man. How does a man find assurance in the deliverance from the sins of his youth (2 Timothy 2:22)?

Instead of keeping score, struggle to defeat sin (1 Corinthians 10:13). The wise man asks, "Is this my best play?" What will life look like on the other side of this temptation? Where is God in this? Read the last page of your story. Play the movie of your life. Know the final score before the game even starts. Play the game before the game plays you.

Sin is not a number.

Sin is not a game.

Refuse to play it.

LAP DANCE

Can a man scoop fire into his lap without his clothes being burned?
Proverbs 6:27

Does the title of today's entry bother you? It should. Years ago, a man and his wife insisted on meeting with me ASAP. Knowing this couple, their faithful years in service, and their love for the Lord, I met with them. She looked numb and pale.

Something was definitely wrong!

He calmly confessed, "Last week I was fired from my job for looking at pornography at work and masturbating." He went on to describe his secret life, and was openly thankful he didn't have to hide it anymore. His story is like thousands of Christian men today who hide their sin behind a secret veil. Most men I know battle the demon of lust. I do. But we must protect ourselves from the many temptations offered through technology—specifically—the Internet. A man is foolish, inviting problems, if he isn't building guardrails against temptation. A man cannot avoid women, but he can avoid scooping the sin of lust into his lap.

In Matthew 5:27-28 Jesus went so far as to say that looking lustfully at a woman is a betrayal against one's wife!

Don't engage in a lap dance with lust.

A man can't be passive when it comes to lust. He must bring his sin into the light and rid himself of any secrecy revolving around the fires of lust. Find trustworthy men and lock arms with them in your battle against lust.

Be open. Be vulnerable. Confess your sins and your temptations. Sin is not a game.

REBOUND EFFECT

For though a righteous man falls seven times, he rises again...
Proverbs 24:16

A six-foot tall post is not an effective scorer on a high school varsity basketball team. I learned this the hard way. But with a linebacker mentality at two hundred and twenty pounds, I learned the art of doing one thing well—rebounding. Recently, I thought about great rebounders in the Bible.

What do Moses, David, and Samson have in common?

They're Old Testament characters. They led God's people. They stumbled. They killed men. They finished in a positive way. Most of all, they're listed in the Faith Hall of Fame of Hebrews 11.

Can you believe that?

David murdered one of his mighty men to cover up his adultery with that man's wife! Moses murdered an Egyptian, then fled for forty years. Samson had major issues with women. In spite of their depravity they are inductees into God's Faith Hall of Fame.

Why?

Because these men lived out Proverbs 24:16, having fallen, they rose again. They rebounded.
This is the rebound effect.

How a man rebounds from failure makes all the difference in the world. These men had a faith so fierce they knew God would receive them back. Look at Peter. His life lacked refinement. He constantly spoke out of place, boasted ignorantly, denied knowing Jesus, and even cut off a man's ear. But Peter bounced back—always.

That's what a man does—he rebounds. He repents. He learns from his sin. No one is perfect. All men sin (Romans 3:23), but how you rebound after failure makes all the difference in the world.

Will sin slam-dunk you into its pit? Or will you be a man strong enough to rebound?

THE INHERITANCE

A good man leaves an inheritance for his children's children, but a sinner's wealth is stored up for the righteous.
Proverbs 13:22

Today is my deceased grandmother's birthday. I am a beneficiary of my grandparent's inheritance. Grandpa Ramos worked hard in construction all his working life and left a large inheritance. He was a good man. He was a Proverbs 13:22 man.

My other grandpa became an alcoholic to cope as a P-51 Mustang pilot during World War II. He was never able to get The War out of his mind or bottle. War memories haunted him, even after he stepped out of the airplane. He ended his career being forced out of the banking industry due to his addiction. He left a small nest egg behind, but one we'll probably never see. He was a good man with a bad problem.

I have another friend whose in-laws joke that their goal in life is to spend every penny and leave exactly zero for their children and grandchildren. Biblically, this is an unwise idea.

A good man sees beyond his possessions. He sees the invisible. He sees the legacy of the wealth he will pass down to his grandchildren. A good man has a succession plan. Even when times are tight a good man has a solid plan to build wealth.

Do you?

Plan for tomorrow.

Have a financial plan that sees beyond your life. Get out of debt now and never look back (Romans 13:8). I love what John Wesley wisely advised, "Earn all you can, give all you can, save all you can."

This is a good rule to live by—earn, give and save.

TEAM MEETING THREE: NO SECRETS

> *"We few, we happy few, we band of brothers. For he today that sheds his blood with me shall be my brother."*
> ~William Shakespeare

What did you take away from last week's study and daily readings? What are you still processing? What challenged your current paradigm? What inspired you to grow as a man?

The book of First John was written to refute a First Century heresy called Gnosticism. Gnosticism was built on a Greek philosophy that taught matter was evil and the spirit was good. This dualistic teaching promoted a clear separation between the material and spiritual world.

Gnostics concluded, since matter was evil, God couldn't be incarnate in a human body. Jesus only "appeared" to be in human form and only "appeared" to suffer. In other words—the crucifixion was an illusion.

Two extremes naturally appeared out of Gnosticism. One was of total gluttony—ignoring the body's health—since the human body being material, was inherently evil. The other Gnostic philosophy practiced extreme discipline to punish the body into complete submission. The first epistle of John was written to refute these extreme views of Gnosticism.

"If we claim to be without sin, we deceive ourselves and the truth is not in us. If we confess our sins, he is faithful and just and will forgive us our sins and purify us from all unrighteousness. If we claim we have not sinned, we make him out to be a liar and his word is not in us."
1 John 1:8-10

TEAM MEETING AT A GLANCE

- Opening Prayer, Weekly Announcements
- Personal and Victory Stories
- Each man will share his story — one man per week until all men have shared.
- After all men have shared their personal story, allow time each week for them to share victory stories.
- Weekly Study Closing Prayer
- Closing Prayer

> *"If a man cannot get through to God it is because there is a secret thing he does not intend to give up."*
> ~Oswald Chambers

Today we are taking a hard look at something that has taken a lot of good men out—their secrets. Specifically, we're talking about secret, unrepented sin. Let's camp on 1 John 1:5-10.

This is the message we have heard from him and declare to you: God is light; in him there is there is no darkness at all. If we claim to have fellowship with him and yet walk in the darkness, we lie and do not live out the truth. But if we walk in the light, as he is in the light, we have fellowship with one another, and the blood of Jesus, his Son, purifies us from all sin. If we claim to be without sin, we deceive ourselves and the truth is not in us. If we confess our sins, he is faithful and just and will forgive us our sins and purify us from all unrighteousness. If we claim we have not sinned, we make him out to be a liar and his word is not in us.
1 John 1:5-10

What stands out the most in this passage regarding sin? Is there anything new that you learned? Do you have any questions?

The Greek word for fellowship mentioned in 1 John 1:6 and 7 is *koinonia*. How does fellowship interact with how we walk with God? Is fellowship more of an event or a process? Share examples of regular fellowship in your life?
John 13:34-35, Romans 12:9-11, Galatians 5:13-14, Ephesians 4:1-3, 14-16, 29-32, and Hebrews 10:23-25

> *"We have no middle ground, no foggy gray area where we can sin a little without suffering spiritual decline. That is why we must repent and come to Christ daily on submissive knees so that we can prevent our bonfires of testimony from being snuffed out by sin."*
> ~Joseph B. Wirthlin

"*Koinonia* is a transliterated form of the Greek word, κοινωνία, which means communion, joint participation; the share which one has in anything, participation, a gift jointly contributed, a collection, a contribution, etc. It identifies the idealized state of fellowship and unity that should exist within the Christian church, the Body of Christ."
~Wikipedia

What contrasts do you see between walking in the darkness (1 John 1:6) and walking in the light (1 John 1:7)? How does the lifestyle of light and darkness differ? How are they similar?

The word "walking" in the Bible describes something that happens regularly in our life—a habit. It describes an established rhythm or ongoing process. When The Great Hunt for God uses the acrostic W.A.L.K.I.N.G. with God we mean:
- Worshipping God on a regular basis,
- Approaching God daily in prayer,
- Loving other believers in regular fellowship,
- Knowing the Word of God,
- Investing tangible resources in Kingdom ministries,
- Nurturing others in the discipleship process, and
- Giving our lives in Christian service for Kingdom causes.

Notice the progressive tense of the verbs. Walking with God is a rhythm or process more than an event.

What does 1 John 1:8 teach us about sin? What excuses surround the man living in secret sin? How do you navigate around the gray areas of drugs/alcohol, money/possessions, sex/lust, and others? At what point does a gray area go entirely dark?
Romans 6:1-6, 1 Corinthians 6:11-13, 10:12-14, James 1:14-16, 4:16-17, and 2 Peter 2:19-20

> *"He that is down needs fear no fall."*
> ~John Bunyan

Look at 1 John 1:9-10. How does confessing secret sin invite others into our field of vision? How does it bring our darkness into the light? How does fellowship help others identify blind spots and deceit in our lives? Who have you invited into your life?
Numbers 5:6-7, 2 Chronicles 7:13-15, and James 5:13-16

We can learn from a lot from our Catholic brothers regarding the sacrament of confession. Confession is manly. Confession is an incredible weapon in our arsenal. Stop believing the lie that you have to protect your tough-guy-veneer. That reasoning doesn't make you more of a man and less of a joke. It makes you more of a joke and less of a man.

Why is confession so tough? What does our refusal to confess say about God? What does it say about you? What do we have to deal with before we confess?
Job 20:6-7, Psalm 10:3-5, Proverbs 16:18, James 4:5-7, 1 John 2:15-17, and 1 Peter 5:4-6

How is confession a game-changer? How have you found the peace and strength to serve God through confession? Excusing ourselves from sin not only discredits God, but who we claim to be as a follower of Jesus. What does 1 John 1:10 mean by, "We make him out to be a liar and his word is not in us"?
1 John 2:3-5, 2:21-23, 4:19-20, and 5:9-11
"If you excuse yourself from confession, you shut up sin within your soul, and shut out pardon."
Augustine
What are your thoughts on the statement, "Our sin matters to God"?
Proverbs 28:13, 1 Corinthians 4:5, and Galatians 6:7-8

Break into groups of three or four.

Do you have a dark side you'd like to confess and receive prayer for?

Take a moment today and pray for each other.

> *"Sacrifice, discipline and prayer are essential. We gain strength through God's word. We receive grace from the sacrament. And when we fumble due to sin— and it's gonna happen— confession puts us back on the field."*
> ~Lou Holtz

STUDY NOTES

_____
_____
_____
_____
_____
_____
_____
_____
_____
_____
_____
_____
_____

For the next five days, read the following entries from our **The Field Guide: A Bathroom Book for Men.**

We hope they challenge and encourage you to get in the great Arena for God. See you on the Arena Floor!

CROSSING OVER

When I was a child, I talked like a child, I thought like a child, I reasoned like a child.
When I became a man, I put childish ways behind me.
1 Corinthians 13:11

My crossing into manhood occurred at a Los Angeles, California Promise Keepers event in 1995. My marriage was struggling, largely due to my immaturity. After hearing a black preacher scream repeatedly, "You've got to out-love and out-serve your wife!," it finally sunk in.

Alone in the Los Angeles Coliseum I decided to out-love and out-serve Shanna for the rest of our lives. I was a thirty-year-old father, husband, and pastor the day I became a man. A man is as a man does.

Manhood isn't chronological. It's deeper than a timeline, facial hair, or the ability to fight for one's country. It's about talking, thinking, and living like a man. It took three decades for me to cross over from boy to man.

Paul ends 1 Corinthians 13 (the Love chapter) with the words every man should read in verse 11. First, a man talks like a man. He listens, avoids gossip, slander, and maliciousness. He's accountable for his words (Matthew 12:34-36), and chooses them wisely.

Second, he thinks like a man. He guards his mind (Philippians 4:6-8) and tests everything he watches, listens to, or reads. He knows that he's only as strong as his mind—guarding it diligently.

Third, he reasons like a man. A male measures life by "my" for "my" and an eye for an eye. A male lives in the here and now unable to process the big picture. To reason like a man is to play every action to its conclusion.

When a man talks, thinks, and reasons like a man, he has crossed over from boyhood to manhood—from male to man.

Are you a male? Or, are you respected as the man you are?

SIN IN THE CAMP

But a man of God came to him and said, "O king, these troops from Israel must not march with you, for the Lord is not with Israel—not with any of the people of Ephraim. Even if you go and fight courageously in battle, God will overthrow you before the enemy, for God has the power to help or to overthrow."
2 Chronicles 25:7-8

Sin in the camp creates a dark cloud over the believer—or church body— regardless of resources or vision (Joshua 7:11). Sin in the camp jeopardizes God's blessing.

Under the leadership of Amaziah, Judah was ready to fight. We read that they were "strong in battle" yet God was about to "bring them down before the enemy" (NASB).

Why? Because God removed His blessing. Leaders take pride in their ability to build momentum in a movement of God. It's tragic when God removes His hand from that movement due to hidden sin. It soon becomes an organization dependent on emotional gimmicks and hype more than ruthless trust in the Creator of the universe.

Trust me. I've seen it before.

God isn't needed if large crowds are a church's primary goal. When we fight for God's movement, our weapons are not of this world. We can't win spiritual battles with worldly weapons. It's God who "has the power to help or bring us down."

When partnering in God's work, look for those who are sold out for the cause of Jesus Christ and white hot for Him. It's better to have average men with passionate hearts, than great men with average hearts. I'll take big-hearted men every time.

God can turn average talent into championship performance by His blessing alone!

Look at your inner circle. Are they passionately pursuing Him? Look at your life. Is there sin in your camp that's robbing you from God's blessing?

WAR AGAINST GOD

"Teacher," they said, "we know you are a man of integrity
I myself will fight against you with an outstretched hand and a mighty arm in anger and fury and great wrath.
Jeremiah 21:5

The American Church has some misconceptions about God. We've transformed God into a gentle giant—a god who is desperate for love. Our treatment of God is more like a jolly Santa Claus and less as the Sovereign King.

We've thrown out the warrior God of the Old Testament and replaced Him with the Jell-O Jesus New Testament god who is soft, gentle, and nice. The "g" is not capitalized because this Jesus is not the God of the Bible. But, the God of war is still the God of love. The God of grace is still the God of wrath. The God of judgment is still the God of mercy. The dilemma comes in trying to balance the two.

Overemphasize the Old Testament and God becomes an angry God of wrath, leading to fundamentalism, hatred, and legalism.

A lopsided focus on the New Testament's God of grace manifests itself in wimpy spirituality, emasculated manhood, and a Jesus who is okay with us fitting Him into our mold.

Before Christ we were "enemies of God" and "objects of wrath" (Ephesians 2:3). In Jeremiah 21:5 we're warned that rebellion against God is a declaration of "war against you" (NASB) pouring out His "anger and wrath and great indignation." Does that sound like a Jell-O Jesus to you?

Me neither.

The war for men was won at the cross, but the battle over their sin rages on with God on the front lines.

Trust me, don't turn your back on this God. Instead reflect on this: "Work out your salvation with fear and trembling" (Philippians 2:12).

SLICK ROCK

Timothy, my son, I give you this instruction in keeping with the prophecies once made about you, so that by following them you may fight the good fight, holding on to faith and a good conscience.
1 Timothy 1:18-19

I once mountain biked the popular Slick Rock Trail in Moab, Utah. The sixteen-mile loop is famous for being all rock. In our family, it's famous for the story I'm hesitant to share.

It was already over one hundred degrees in the early morning as I pedaled away from my car. Overly confident, I failed to plan for the heat and was quickly out of water. As the heat climbed my hydration levels dropped and after an hour I was completely dehydrated and could barely pedal. I was in trouble. I bonked. Thankfully a fellow biker (and EMT) shared his water and coached me out of the desert in one piece.

It's hard to survive without water, especially in the desert where resources are scarce. We thirst, but water is nowhere to be found. We're isolated, but every oasis is a dead end. Paul encouraged his protégé, Timothy to "fight the good fight." Fighting is easy when well supplied—but much different in the desert!

We don't need to be encouraged when the stomach is full and life is good. We need it when our tank is empty and we're ready to quit. Being a man is tough. You'll want to throw in the towel—many do. Don't be numbered among the males of this world. Instead, lock arms with men who'll push you when you can't push anymore.

Men wrongly assume that their fights will be under good conditions. This couldn't be further from the truth. Conditions are rarely perfect. God led Jesus into the Desert of Temptation (Matthew 4:1-11). He'll be with you in The Valley of the Shadow of Death (Psalm 23).

Those who finish strong have learned the art of navigating in the desert. It's where the metal of manhood is forged.

A BATTLE RANT

So he said, "Do you know why I have come to you? Soon I will return to fight against the prince of Persia, and when I go, the prince of Greece will come; but first I will tell you what is written in the Book of Truth. (No one supports me against them except Michael, your prince.)"
Daniel 10:20-21

Some songs are timeless. One of those is Toby Keith's 'Courtesy of the Red, White, and Blue' (The Angry American), written in response to the terrorist attack of September 11, 2001. Listen to the emotion in these words:

"Now this nation that I love has fallen under attack, a mighty sucker punch came flying in from somewhere in the back. Soon as we could see clearly through our big black eye, man, we lit up your world like the 4th of July!"

Studying the word fight in Scripture it becomes clear that there's a vicious spiritual war in the heavenly realms (Daniel 10:20-21). Jesus alluded to it, "The kingdom of heaven has been forcefully advancing, and forceful men lay hold of it" (Matthew 11:12).

Valiant soldiers who've bled for this country have protected American lands. Except for a few instances, American soil has experienced peace for more than a hundred years. But to believe it will last simply reveals our spoiled American attitudes.

To quote author Stu Weber, "We live in the era of the soft male." It's easy to say you're anti-war, holding posters on street corners during times of peace. It is much different when that peace is threatened and it's either fight or die a coward's death.

Be willing to receive persecution unto death for your faith as a badge of honor, but it's the Christian's duty to fight and defend the weak, powerless, and those we're called to protect.

TEAM MEETING FOUR: MEN ON THE ROOF

> *"I hate and regret the failure of my marriages. I would gladly give all my millions for just one lasting marital success."*
> ~ J. Paul Getty

What did you take away from last week's study and daily readings? What are you still processing? What challenged your current paradigm? What inspired you to grow as a man?

Friends Rick Talbott and Mike Mingay inspired today's meeting, "Men on the Roof", taken from Mark 2:1-5 (below). Rick and Mike prayed together about a theme for their church's men's retreat and were convinced that I teach on the topic, "Men on the Roof." The weekend was so impactful that I was compelled to ask, "Who are the men on my roof?"

Last week we spoke to you about exposing secret sin and the power of confession. Confession is manly. When a man confesses to a trusted band of brothers he exposes his darkness and brings it into the light. Today we're discussing the effects of isolation on a man. Men usually err on the side of isolation, which is not a biblical principle. Isolation leads to a desolation and sets us up as prey for a patient and extremely effective predator. Read the story highlighting some heroic men on the roof found in Mark 2:1-5.

And when he returned to Capernaum after some days, it was reported that he was at home. And many were gathered together, so that there was no more room, not even at the door and he was preaching the word to them. And they came, bringing to him a paralytic carried by four men. And when they could not get near him because of the crowd, they removed the roof above him, and when they had made an opening, they let down the bed on which the paralytic lay. And when Jesus saw their faith, he said to the paralytic, "Son, your sins are forgiven."
Mark 2:1-5 (ESV)

TEAM MEETING AT A GLANCE

- Opening Prayer, Weekly Announcements
- Personal and Victory Stories
- Each man will share his story — one man per week until all men have shared.
- After all men have shared their personal story, allow time each week for them to share victory stories.
- Weekly Study Closing Prayer
- Closing Prayer

> *"Don't ask yourself what the world needs. Ask yourself what makes you come alive, and then go do that. Because what the world needs is people who have come alive."*
> ~Harold Thurman Whitman

What stands out in this story? How many men were involved in lowering their friend to Jesus? Who watched the stairs? Who dug the hole in the roof ? Who held their buddy up and lowered him down? Who caught him at the bottom? Read verse three carefully before you answer.

"The roof of a Palestine house was flat. It was regularly used for a place of rest and quiet, and so usually there was an outside stair, which ascended to it. The construction of the roof lent it to what these ingenious four proposed to do. The roof consisted of flat beams laid across from wall to wall, perhaps three feet apart. The space in between the beams was filled with brushwood packed tight with clay. The top was then made watertight. Very largely the roof was of earth and often the flourishing crop of grass grew on the roof of a Palestinian house. It was the easiest thing in the world to dig out the filling between the two beams; it did not even damage the house very much, and it was easy to repair the breach again. So the four men dug out the filling between two of the beams and let their friend down directly at Jesus's feet."
~William Barclay

Look at Mark 2:1-5 one more time. Whose faith does this story tell us was the catalyst for the man's healing? What does this tell you about the men on the roof in your life? Why do we need others to grow as men of God?
Mark 2:6-12 and Luke 5:17-26

> *"Don't judge what you don't know about me based only on what you know about yourself."*
> ~Mike Yaconelli,
> Youth Specialties Founder

At some point in life we all need hole diggers, stretcher carriers, catchers, and stair watchers to experience a breakthrough. The men on the roof in my life are guys that deconstruct all barriers hindering me from total freedom in Jesus. They carry me when I can't carry myself. They have faith when I can't muster my own. They truly have my back.

Read Mark 2:1-12 again. What reason does Mark offer readers for why these friends lowered him? How is Luke 5:17-26 different? Did these friends lower their buddy to hear Jesus, be healed by Jesus, or a combination of both?

Most scholars agree that Mark's gospel was written through Peter's eyes. In other words, Mark was Peter's translator. The theme of Mark is "Jesus the human, focusing on the human side of Jesus. Nowhere does Mark mention the men on the roof wanting Jesus to heal their friend. Instead, it can be argued that they simply wanted their buddy to hear Jesus' teachings.

Mark 2:2 simply records that, "They gathered in such large numbers that there was no room left, not even outside the door, and he preached the word to them." Luke 5:17-26, however, mentions that the friends wanted their friend healed. It's also interesting that Jesus doesn't immediately heal him. He forgave him first and healed him almost as an afterthought.

Who are the men on the roof with you? Would they say the same about you? Why are these men so vital to your faith? How have they changed your life? Why are deep and authentic relationships so crucial?

George Vaillant was the study director for Harvard University's Grant Study tracking 268 physically and mentally healthy (white, American) male college sophomores (20 years old) at Harvard University born in 1919-1924. He tracked them over seventy-five years. The enduring men continue to be studied. The men were evaluated at least every two years by questionnaires, information from their physicians, and in many cases by personal interviews.

Information was gathered about their mental and physical health, career enjoyment, retirement experience and marital quality. The goal of the study was to identify predictors of healthy aging. Vaillant writes, "It was the capacity for intimate relationships that predicted the flourishing aspects of these men's lives."

Thirty-one men of the men were incapable of forming intimate relationships. Only four were alive in 2014. Essentially, the men who isolated themselves from others died sooner! "The study found strong relationships to be far and away the strongest predictor of life satisfaction. And in terms of career satisfaction, too, feeling connected to one's work was far more important than making money or achieving traditional success."
~Huffington Post

Of those better at forming relationships, over one-third were still alive. In case after case, the magic formula is the capacity for intimacy combined with persistence, discipline, order, and dependability.

How is isolation dangerous? When is isolation the most destructive? How do natural predators use isolation to their advantage? How does the enemy use isolation as one of his greatest tools?
John 13:34-45, Galatians 6:1-2, and Hebrews 10:23-25

It's not always so easy to recognize Satan, the predator (and his allies), especially when we've strayed. The predator is a master of disguise going to extreme measures to cause us to stray from God and His people. Like the killer he is, he preys upon the young and immature, sick and dying weak and wounded, and proud and isolated.

His strategy is to separate you from the safety and protection of fellowship. He is the most patient of predators, waiting for decades if need be. Then—when the time is right—he'll take you out.

> *"There are two ways of spreading light: to be the candle or the mirror that reflects it."*
> ~ Edith Wharton

Does Satan exist? How do you know? How does this evil predator use camouflage to his advantage? What are some other strategies he uses?
Matthew 7:15-16, John 10:10, 2 Corinthians 11:13-15, and 1 Peter 5:5-9

In 2010, The Barna Group Surveyed that 40% of Christians strongly agreed that Satan, "is not a living being but is a symbol of evil." An additional two out of ten Christians (19%) said they "agree somewhat" with that perspective. A minority of Christians indicated that they believe Satan is real by disagreeing with the statement: one-quarter (26%) disagreed strongly and about one-tenth (9%) disagree somewhat. The remaining 8% were not sure what they believe about the existence of Satan.

A war is waging between two very real shepherds. One will never stop loving you. The other will never stop lying to you. One wants you to stay with Him. The other wants you to stray towards him. One is The Good Shepherd. One is an evil shepherd. One is a Protector; one a predator. Can you identify any areas in your life where you have been deceived away from truth? What isolating lies have you believed? Where have you isolated yourself from deep and authentic relationships with potential men on your roof? What relationships are hurting you and how do you fix them?
Proverbs 22:3, Ecclesiastes 12:13-14, Matthew 24:4-5, John 8:44, and Galatians 6:7-8

Birds of a feather. Water seeks its own level.

The Association Principle teaches that birds of a feather flock together, water seeks its own level, and like begets like. If the men you've invited up on the roof are hindering your growth, then either find new men for your inner circle or don't stay in the same place. We are the way we are and are becoming, in part, because of the people we have on the roof. It's really that simple.

Satan, the master predator he is, prowls around waiting for us to stray. How do we resist his plot to isolate us from men on the roof ?
Luke 21:14-16, Ephesians 6:11, Hebrews 12:3-5, 1 Peter 5:9, and James 4:7

Break into groups of three or four.

Who are your men on the roof ? What are their names? Would they agree with you?

Take a moment today and pray for each other.

> *"A rising tide lifts all boats."*
> ~John F. Kennedy

STUDY NOTES

For the next five days, read the following entries from our **The Field Guide: A Bathroom Book for Men.**

We hope they challenge and encourage you to get in the great Arena for God. See you on the Arena Floor!

COINCIDENCES

The race is not to the swift or the battle to the strong, nor does food come to the wise or wealth to the brilliant or favor to the learned; but time and chance happen to them all.
Ecclesiastes 9:11

Think of the famous men seen in the media today: the athletes, businessmen, commentators, and movie stars. Who comes to your mind? Do any publicly confess Jesus as Lord of their lives? If you're like me, most of you answered, "No" for most (if not all) of them.

How did they achieve their fame and fortune? Did God somehow bless them and not others? Is it simply blind luck?

Until recently, my answer would've been a Christian cliché like, "There are no coincidences with God." Or, "Christians don't believe in luck." Ecclesiastes 9:11, quite frankly, has me scratching my bald head. What if chance exists? What if coincidence is a reality? If I don't believe in chance, luck, or coincidence, I'm forced to believe that God blesses those who reject Him.

What if God ignores insignificant things such as worldly success, athleticism, and fame? What if natural laws are allowed to play out through choice and genetics?

I know God is all-powerful, and I firmly believe He's sovereign. But what if Solomon was right, "that time and chance happen to them all"? What if coincidence co-exists with blind luck and chance? They have to. Why would God bless those who ignore Him, unless success simply comes through God-given ability, choices, or work ethic?

But we must never ignore the fact that every man—successful or not— will face his Maker and give an account for who received the glory for his ability, choices, and work ethic (Hebrews 9:27).

RECKLESS ABANDON

"Be strong, do not fear; your God will come...
Isaiah 35:4

The thief comes only to steal and kill and destroy; I have come that they may have life, and have it to the full.
John 10:10

Thanks to my wife's loving push, I tried snowboarding. Actually, it was closer to snow falling or snow plowing. A two-hundred-fifty-pound-man flying uncontrollably down an ice-covered mountain should be illegal. I could have seriously hurt someone.

The reason I disliked snowboarding was the feeling of total loss of control. During those times when fear confined me to the comforts of the lodge—Shanna would stare me down and say, "Is this living out your life verse?" I hate when she does that. Back to the ski lift.

I want to live a life without regrets, huge lapses in judgment, or massive scheduling gaps that waste time. I don't want to get to the end and regret the choices I've made.

Choose the ski lift over the lodge. Choose living your dreams over game stations. Choose coffee with friends over social networking. Choose playing with your children over watching television with them.

Go to bed last.

Wake up first.

American kickboxer, Joe Lewis (March 7, 1944-August 31, 2012) once said, "We only have one life to live but if we do it right, once is enough." Failure is a life of regret, wishing for a do-over. Don't live today in a way that would cause you to regret your life later.

You get one shot at this.

Exploit life. Live it to the fullest. The only way to soar is to connect to the Source (John 15:1-8). Life is much more than existence.

It's living with reckless abandon.

IDOLS FROM THE PAST

Now fear the Lord and serve him with all faithfulness. Throw away the gods your forefathers worshiped beyond the River and in Egypt, and serve the Lord. But if serving the Lord seems undesirable to you, then choose for yourselves this day whom you will serve, whether the gods your forefathers served beyond the River, or the gods of the Amorites, in whose land you are living. But as for my household, and me we will serve the Lord.
Joshua 24:14-15

I love to laugh out loud and exploit the phrase, "The older I get the better I was." It's easy to brag about a past we can't prove, making ourselves larger than life and truth.

What about the men who brag about their sinful past like a badge of honor? These men concern me. Past sin is something to be ashamed of not put on a pedestal and bragged about like a trophy.

I'm intrigued by a man's last words. Parting words express the true heart. Today we look at Joshua's. You may have heard the saying, "You can say anything on your last day." But it would be wiser to live by the axiom "Never say anything on your last day you'll regret." Of all great things he could've said, Joshua chose to encourage the people to "Fear the Lord and serve him with all faithfulness."

Negatively, those who fear the Lord must "throw away the gods of your forefathers."Except for Caleb and Joshua the exodus generation died, but their idols remained. Maybe they were passed down. Maybe they were discovered among their parents' belongings. The idols endured into the Promised Land—a symbol of rebellion. How often we brag about the sins of our past, like an idol we've tucked away.

How often do men share their testimony only to spend more time bragging about their sin than their God? These men have made their past an idol. Positively, those who fear the Lord are told twice to "serve the Lord." To fear Him is to serve Him. The man who serves God destroys the idols of his past because they're worthless compared to knowing the one true God.

SHRINK TO FIT

*But we do not belong to those who shrink back and are destroyed,
but to those who have faith and are saved.*
Hebrews 10:39

On New Year's Eve his wife went into premature labor. Still leading a team of missionaries, they rushed her to the hospital where she delivered a beautiful baby girl. She was perfect.

Perfect, except her tiny body couldn't survive, and moments later she slipped into eternity while in her daddy's arms.

I sat speechless staring into the Caribbean Ocean as this missionary dad shared his story only months after the tragic event.

How do I comfort this young man? What can I say? What wisdom can I offer? Heck, I'm the speaker this week. I should know what to do! Instead, it was his words that comforted me. With two weeks left on their mission, this mourning couple chose to stay and lead their team to its conclusion. They chose to finish strong when quitting would have been accepted—even applauded.

Then he told me why. "Someone encouraged me with Hebrews 10:39." I drew a blank.

"It says," he continued, "But we do not belong to those who shrink back and are destroyed, but to those who have faith and are saved. We decided even though we were hurting we wouldn't shrink back. Instead we would finish our mission with the team we were leading."

With his words, I knew I was on holy ground.

Shrinking back is normal today—stepping up—not so much. Males shrink back. Men step up. They never shrink back. While males are busy making socially acceptable excuses, men are busy stepping up. Never shrink back. Always step up.
Be a man.

POURED OUT

But even if I am being poured out like a drink offering on the sacrifice and service coming from your faith, I am glad and rejoice with all of you.
Philippians 2:17

Exhausted after one high school football game, I walked into the showers and vomited uncontrollably. It was gross. Apparently you can drink too much Gatorade.

Talk about pouring yourself out. I didn't leave it all on the field. I left some of it in the shower too! Disgusting! It's a reminder of today's passage. God asks men to pour themselves out on Christ's behalf. A man's life is a sacrificial offering for some greater, larger-than-life calling. God makes the man who seeks Him bigger than he thinks he is as he relies on God's help by faith. Remember, God wants to put you on display. But there's a price to pay. That price is sacrifice.

What are you pouring yourself into?

Leave it all on the field or lose it all in the shower.

It's your choice. Are you a fake? Are you a poser? Do you pace yourself just enough to look like a player, but you're not performing at full capacity? How committed are you?

Really?

Commitment only flows through one valve. Commitment is not wide spray from a nozzle but a focused jet stream. It's not a light but a laser beam. Refuse to count yourself with those anonymous men who are satisfied with less than focused commitment. Leave it all on the field.

Live your life well.

Go hard.

Pour it on.

TEAM MEETING FIVE: COVENANT EYES

> *"(Lust is) a strong feeling of sexual desire: a strong desire for something."*
> ~Simple Definition of Lust, Merriam-Webster

What did you take away from last week's study and daily readings? What are you still processing? What challenged your current paradigm? What inspired you to grow as a man?

When I was a single man in my twenties, my friend and youth ministry mentor, the late Rich Fisher, shared something I never forgot. They're words I live by to this day. Using basketball terminology, he said, "You have three seconds in the key. You have exactly three seconds to admire a beautiful woman. After that it's a foul."

This meeting is dedicated to you my friend, Rich Fisher—until we meet again, my friend. Share one rule you have to prevent your eyes from wandering into lust?

Memorize Job 31:1. What does this verse mean? When do you know that you've crossed from admiration of a beautiful woman to lusting after her?
Proverbs 17:24

> *"I made a covenant with my eyes not to look lustfully at a young woman.*
> Job 31:1

What did Jesus mean in Matthew 5:28 by, "But I tell you that anyone who looks at a woman lustfully has already committed adultery with her in his heart." Where do you draw the line with your eyes?

54

TEAM MEETING AT A GLANCE

- Opening Prayer, Weekly Announcements
- Personal and Victory Stories
- Each man will share his story — one man per week until all men have shared.
- After all men have shared their personal story, allow time each week for them to share victory stories.
- Weekly Study Closing Prayer
- Closing Prayer

> *"Lose the sex battle and defeat spreads into every portion of your being."*
> ~E Stanley Jones

You have heard that it was said, 'You shall not commit adultery.' But I say to you that everyone who looks at a woman with lustful intent has already committed adultery with her in his heart. If your right eye causes you to sin, tear it out and throw it away. For it is better that you lose one of your members than that your whole body be thrown into hell.
Matthew 5:27-29 (ESV)

The Greek word for "lust" is epithymia. Look up the following scripture translations of epithymia. What other words are used to describe lust?
Romans 13:9, Galatians 5:24, Ephesians 2:3, 4:22, Colossians 3:5-6, and Titus 2:12

"Lust (*epithymia*) is strong craving or desire, often of a sexual nature. Though used relatively infrequently (twenty-nine times) in Scripture, a common theme can be seen running through its occurrences. The word is never used in a positive context; rather, it is always seen in a negative light, relating primarily either to a strong desire for sexual immorality or idolatrous worship.

> *"A pair of breasts can pull a man further then a pair of oxen ever can."*
> ~Rev. Bufe Karraker

> *"He that but looketh on a plate of ham and eggs to lust after it hath already committed breakfast with it in his heart."*
> ~ C.S. Lewis

The Greek word *epithymia* can be used in a neutral or good sense (Matthew 13:17). In these instances, the New International Version does not translate the word as lust. Rather, it is translated as desire, longing, and the like. The context surrounding the word lends to this translation in such instances. However, in Scripture, as translated in the New International Version, the word is used for a strong desire that is negative and forbidden.

"Indeed, the unregenerate are governed and controlled by deceitful lusts or desires." ~Biblestudytools.com

How do you control your eyes and thought life? What words of wisdom about your thought life would you pass down to the younger generations? What do the following passages teach about our thought life?
Psalm 90:8, Matthew 9:3-5, Romans 12:1-2, Philippians 4:8-9, and 1 John 2:15-17

If you struggle with what you look at online, protect your electronic devices and visit www.covenanteyes.com today.

"Whether we fall by ambition, blood, or lust, like diamonds we are cut with our own dust." John Webster

What wisdom do the Proverbs pass down to us? How do they profile an adulterous woman? What can you do to avoid her pull?
Proverbs 2:16, 6:23-26, 7:5, 5:3, 22:14, and 30:20

We live in a generation like none other before us. Not only do contemporary men have a myriad of ways to access pornography but sex is unapologetically portrayed in the media. Pornography is an accepted and celebrated norm, and women have become sexual aggressors more than ever. It isn't good enough to guard against lust. A man must also guard himself from all situations that may blindside him with advances by an overly aggressive woman who isn't his wife—and will never be!

> *"Sex is a wonderful servant but a terrible master."*
> ~ E Stanley Jones

What do you find interesting about the last four of the Ten Commandments? What can we gather about our neighbors from this? Exodus 20:14-17 and Deuteronomy 5:18-21

You shall not commit adultery. You shall not steal. You shall not bear false witness against your neighbor. You shall not covet your neighbor's house; you shall not covet your neighbor's wife, or his male servant, or his female servant, or his ox, or his donkey, or anything that is your neighbor's.
Exodus 20:14-17 (ESV)

Why should you guard against people you are close to such as a neighbor's wife, co-worker, or best friend's significant other? What truth is there in the phrase, "You can't trust your best friend"?

Break into groups of three or four.

Where are you struggling with your thought life?

Is there another woman who has caught your eye to the degree that you may have crossed a line?

Take a moment today and pray for each other.

STUDY NOTES

For the next five days, read the following entries from our **The Field Guide: A Bathroom Book for Men.**

We hope they challenge and encourage you to get in the great Arena for God. See you on the Arena Floor!

GREAT SACRIFICES

He told them, "Consider carefully what you do, because you are not judging for mere mortals but for the Lord, who is with you whenever you give a verdict. Now let the fear of the LORD be upon you. Judge carefully, for with the LORD our God there is no injustice or partiality or bribery."
2 Chronicles 19:6-7

But now he has appeared once for all at the end of the ages to do away with sin by the sacrifice of himself.
Hebrews 9:26

The Marines have a saying that, "Pain is weakness leaving the body." Pain is a part of life.

Pain is a part of sacrifice. Without pain, sacrifice can't exist. Pain is a characteristic of sacrifice. The Bible teaches that pain is sacrifice leaving our selfishness. But there's more to sacrifice then just pain. The greatest sacrifice is dying for a worthy cause. The greater the sacrifice the less it occurs. For example, a man only dies for his country once.

Men love to talk about sacrifice, but talk is cheap without the scars. In his Book of Man, William Bennett writes, "War provokes the highest virtues of a man's soul: honor, fortitude, service, and sacrifice. It is no wonder that the greatest moments of man are often found in battle." But only one man sacrificed himself for humanity, "For Christ died for sins once for all, the righteous for the unrighteous, to bring you to God" (1 Peter 3:18). The sacrifice of Christ is the greatest because it can't be duplicated. It stands alone as the single greatest act of sacrifice. It's the one sacrifice that has the power to "do away with sin" (Hebrews 9:26).

The sacrifice of Christ gives Him the seat of honor at "the right hand of God" (Hebrews 10:12).

One day, "every knee will bow" (Philippians 2:10) to pay honor to the ultimate sacrifice. It's so great a sacrifice it has the unique power to make those who receive it "perfect forever". (Hebrews 10:14).

ONE FOR THE TEAM

He himself bore our sins in his body on the tree, so that we might die to sins and live for righteousness; by his wounds you have been healed.
1 Peter 2:24

Taking the charge in basketball.

Laying out to block a field goal in football.

Getting hit by the pitcher in baseball.

Taking a header at the net in soccer.

Allowing a teammate to draft behind you in a bike race.

Each of these is an example of sacrifice. Sacrifice takes one for the team. It's when an athlete is willing to sacrifice his advantage for the team's greater good. In sports, that greater good is winning. Sacrificial athletes epitomize the cliché, "There's no 'I' in team."

Listen to Jesus in this passage: "Sacrifice and offering you did not desire, but a body you prepared for me" (Hebrews 10:5).

A what?

You heard it correctly, "The Word became flesh and made his dwelling among us" (John 1:14).

He became the last sacrifice for the sins of all—Jesus took one for the team. The sacrifices made by men could never cleanse the human race of its sin.

Only God can do that.

Hebrews 10:10 confirms this with, "We have been made holy through the sacrifice of the body of Jesus Christ once for all."

Talk about taking one for the team!

Jesus took the charge, drafted the wind, and leaned into the pitch. Best of all, he did it as a "forever" sacrifice on our behalf.

STICKERS

And where these have been forgiven, there is no longer any sacrifice for sin.
Hebrews 10:18

My college football helmet is prominently displayed in my library. Besides a SC (Santa Clara) sticker on each side, two stickers adorn the back. One is a three-leaf clover honoring Coach Pat Malley who lost his battle with cancer after nearly three decades of leading the Santa Clara Broncos football program.

The other is the number "43," representing a teammate and friend who died tragically after making a game saving tackle. After the memorial service the team, serving as pallbearers, loaded our fallen comrade into the hearse when his weeping father shouted, "Don't let his death be in vain! Don't let his death be in vain!" Later, I understood his words to mean, "Use this tragedy as a tool, not an excuse. Let his sacrifice be the fuel to finish strong."

Sadly, we see Jesus' death in vain when men stubbornly refuse to walk in obedience. To come to Christ yet remain in sin's grasp is to allow Christ's suffering to be in vain. There are three possibilities for the man who—by choice—remains under the darkness of sin. The first is that he never came to Christ at all and is being deceived. He's lost.

Second, the man could be in the healing process. Total healing and sub sequent freedom is seldom instantaneous—there's often a great struggle. The process to overcome sin's stronghold is a battle we all fight at some time.

Third, the man is just obstinate. He willfully chooses to walk in darkness even after the chains have been broken.

This man is in grave danger as he mocks the cross of Christ. "If we claim to have fellowship with him yet walk in the darkness, we lie and do not live by the truth" (1 John 1:6). Examine your life. Is there a secret sin that you refuse to repent of? Don't let Christ's death be in vain.

BLOOD BROTHERS

They entered into the covenant to seek the Lord God of their fathers with all their heart and soul.
2 Chronicles 15:12 (NASB)

Years ago, I had the opportunity to hire a college pastor. After the interview process we made a verbal covenant to stick together for at least three years. Nothing was written. There were no lawyers involved. There was no signed contract. The deal was sealed by the word of two men and the power of covenant.

Through the power of covenant and God's grace, three years later, he left a different man—full, rich, and overflowing with God's call upon his life. From today's passage the Israelites formed a covenant to seek God. A covenant is much different than a contract.

A contract acts as a hedge or firewall of protection. It's a veneer guarding a man from total transparency. In the ancient times a covenant was transacted by cutting an animal from top to bottom (Jeremiah 34:18). The covenanting parties then walked through the carcass in a figure eight fashion symbolizing infinity while speaking blessings and curses, based on the fulfillment or breaking of covenant.

Often a cut on the hand of covenanting parties sealed with a handshake would mark the new covenant. The wound would then be treated with dirt to guarantee scarring as a further reminder of covenant.

A tree was sometimes planted as a monument to the covenant made, often followed by a meal, including bread and wine.

Blood, sacrifice, scarred hands, covenant meal, and a tree planted. This sounds strangely familiar to Christ's death.

Maybe it's not so strange at all!

ENDO FOCUS

Glory in his holy name; let the hearts of those who seek the Lord rejoice. Look to the Lord and his strength; seek his face always.
1 Chronicles 16:10-11

As I mountain biked down Manzanita Trail in California's Montana De Oro State Park, I could see the ominous rock in the middle of the trail fifty feet away. A foot high and two-feet long, it stared me down from the center of the trail.

I considered how to avoid it, but it seemed to challenge me. Its magnetism drew me in. Before I knew it, I was flying end-over-end in a textbook mountain bike endo. In our little game of chicken, the rock obviously won. I learned a painful lesson that day.

We'll hit the object of our focus every time. Good or bad, right or wrong, it doesn't matter whether we are trying to avoid it or not—you hit what you aim at.

Try not to lose and you'll lose. Try not to overeat and you'll overeat. Try not to miss the shot and you'll miss. Try not to overreact and, yep…you're getting the point.

You hit where you focus.

Avoiding something adverse can become a focal point. I couldn't take my eyes off it. That rock owned me. The world challenges us with its many options. These options demand focus, often pulling us further from fixing our attention on Christ.

The world offers lots of shiny prizes. The grass looks so much greener to the man who loses focus. But Hebrews 12:2 reminds us to, "Fix our eyes on Jesus the author and perfecter of our faith."

Focus on the right things. Focus on fulfilling your commitments as you focus on the things of God.

TEAM MEETING SIX: BEFORE THE FALL

> "According to Christian teachers, the essential vice, the utmost evil, is Pride. Infidelity, anger, greed, drunkenness, and all that, are mere flea bites in comparison: it was through Pride that the devil became the devil: Pride leads to every other vice: it is the complete anti-God state of mind."
> ~C.S. Lewis, *Mere Christianity*

What did you take away from last week's study and daily readings? What are you still processing? What challenged your current paradigm? What inspired you to grow as a man?

The Trail's End: Finishing Strong is the fifth and final book in The Strong Men Series. Why is overcoming pride such a factor in finishing strong? How does pride hurt a man? Why would C.S. Lewis call it the "anti-God state of mind"?

"*Hubris* from ancient Greek refers to a purely negative emotion that may be defined verbally in a modern context as extreme or foolish pride or confidence. In its ancient Greek context, it typically describes violent behavior rather than an attitude.

The adjectival form of the noun hubris is hubristic. Hubris is usually perceived as a characteristic of an individual rather than a group, although the group the offender belongs to may unintentionally suffer consequences from the wrongful act. Hubris often indicates a loss of contact with reality and an overestimation of one's own competence, accomplishments or capabilities."
~Wikipedia

TEAM MEETING AT A GLANCE

- Opening Prayer, Weekly Announcements
- Personal and Victory Stories
- Each man will share his story — one man per week until all men have shared.
- After all men have shared their personal story, allow time each week for them to share victory stories.
- Weekly Study Closing Prayer
- Closing Prayer

> *"There is not enough darkness in all the world to put out the light of even one small candle."*
> ~Robert Alden

Where do you struggle with pride? How has your pride hurt your relationships? How has pride hindered your relationship with God?

We've heard it said that pride comes before the fall (Proverbs 16:18), but how many relationships have to fall because of our foolish pride before we repent and walk in humility.

When we shame those caught in sin they will change out of shame—for a season. But when we love those caught in sin the chance of true—lasting—repentance is greater. What is the difference between repentance and the shame of being caught? What warning do we find in Galatians 6:1-6?

Brothers, if anyone is caught in any transgression, you who are spiritual should restore him in a spirit of gentleness. Keep watch on yourself, lest you too be tempted. Bear one another's burdens, and so fulfill the law of Christ. For if anyone thinks he is something, when he is nothing, he deceives himself. But let each one test his own work, and then his reason to boast will be in himself alone and not in his neighbor. For each will have to bear his own load. Let the one who is taught the word share all good things with the one who teaches.
Galatians 6:1-6 (ESV)

> *"A man cannot 'finish the course' or say that he's 'kept the faith' until he possesses a win or die attitude that resolves to 'fight the good fight' to his dying end."*
> ~Anonymous

How is the act of shaming a form of pride? What does it say about us? Look at some examples (provided below) where Jesus choose kindness over shame.
John 4:16-26, 39-42, and 8:1-11

"Hubris is to cause shame to the victim, not in order that anything may happen to you, nor because anything has happened to you, but merely for your own gratification. Hubris is not the requital of past injuries; this is revenge. As for the pleasure in hubris, its cause is this: naive men think that by ill-treating others they make their own superiority the greater."
~Aristotle

How do men respond to being shamed? How is shame similar to disrespect? What are some consequences of shame? What are consequences of the person doing the shaming?

Where is the pride when we shame someone simply because their sin struggle is different than ours? How does the process of carrying each other's burdens help to fight against pride and shame?
Proverbs 16:18-19, Matthew 7:1-5, and Galatians 6:1-4

How do you explain the apparent contradiction between Galatians 6:2 and 6:5? How might carrying each other's burden benefit us more than them? How does serving others keep our pride in check?
Psalm 26:1-3, 139:22-24, and Lamentations 3:40-42

> *"There are two kinds of pride, both good and bad. 'Good pride' represents our dignity and self-respect. 'Bad pride' is the deadly sin of superiority that reeks of conceit and arrogance."*
> ~John C. Maxwell

> *"A proud man is always looking down on things and people; and, of course, as long as you're looking down, you can't see something that's above you."*
> ~C.S. Lewis

"Come to me, all you who are weary and burdened, and I will give you rest. Take my yoke upon you and learn from me, for I am gentle and humble in heart, and you will find rest for your souls. For my yoke is easy and my burden is light."
Matthew 11:28-30

Discuss this quote from John R.W. Stott that, "Pride is your greatest enemy, humility is your greatest friend." How is your pride hurting you? How has your pride isolated you from others in relationship? How might it hinder you from finishing strong?

Break into groups of three or four.

Is there an area of your life where you're standing in hubris over a person or group instead of carrying the load?

Take a moment today and pray for each other.

> *"Pride deafens us to the advice or warnings of those around us."*
> ~John C. Maxwell

STUDY NOTES

_____
_____
_____
_____
_____
_____
_____
_____
_____
_____
_____
_____
_____
_____

For the next five days, read the following entries from our **The Field Guide: A Bathroom Book for Men.**

We hope they challenge and encourage you to get in the great Arena for God. See you on the Arena Floor!

THE HUMAN WILL

He gives strength to the weary and increases the power of the weak. Even youths grow tired and weary, and young men stumble and fall; but those who hope in the Lord will renew their strength. They will soar on wings like eagles; they will run and not grow weary, they will walk and not be faint.
Isaiah 40:29-31

I woke up around sunrise on day two at Hume Lake's high school summer camp, but it took twenty minutes to get out of bed. My hamstring ached from yesterday's "capture the fort" paintball war. It served as a painful reminder that I'm not as young as I used to be.

Today's passage encourages all, like myself, who suffer from an aging body. Today's passage revealed a mystery of the spiritual journey as God graciously "increases the power of the weak."
In other words, God takes our aging—and weakening—bodies and empowers us with the spiritual stamina to finish strong.

Even young men get tired. How much more will He strengthen those who are aging? How much more will He strengthen those bearing the battle scars of life?

The aging warriors "who hope in the Lord will renew their strength!" What a promise! Hope is an expectation of faith. It's trust in the fulfillment of a promise. It's the anticipation of something great and wonderful. Hope is the vision of a promise fulfilled before it comes to pass.

Our bodies decay. They get battered over time. They slowly break down. Make the transition from trusting in the strength of your youth to the God of your maturity.

REAL STRENGTH

Therefore we do not lose heart. Though outwardly we are wasting away, yet inwardly we are being renewed day by day.
2 Corinthians 4:16

It took a few months. But when it happened there was no mistake. I'm not sure if the culprit was one too many double-unders on the jump rope, deadlifts, twenty-four-inch box jumps, or kettlebell swings, but when my back blew out I was down for the count.

A herniated disc in my lower back added to my portfolio of injuries. Almost two years, a failed back surgery, and not a single pain-free day later, today's passage hits close to home.

Many learn the hard way that physical stamina diminishes with age. But "we do not lose heart" though, "outwardly we are wasting away" because hopefully, "inwardly we are being renewed day by day."

Our finite bodies are just "momentary troubles" that must be endured until we reach "eternal glory" when our soul will supersede our bodies in victory. A question I struggle with at fifty is, "How do I renew my spirit in the midst of a decaying body?"

Today's passage is our answer. "Fix our eyes not on what is seen but on what is unseen. For what is seen is temporary but what is unseen is eternal" (2 Corinthians 4:18). It's about focus.

It's about trusting in that which never breaks down or decays. True strength is found when we separate the eternal from the temporal (Jeremiah 15:19-20). It's being fixated on the cross.

It's being focused on eternity instead of a decaying body.

LIVING AND DYING

All our days pass away under your wrath;
we finish our years with a moan.
The length of our days is seventy years—or eighty,
if we have the strength;
yet their span is but trouble and sorrow,
for they quickly pass, and we fly away.
Psalm 90:9-10

Yesterday I shared about a severe back injury that occurred while— ironically—exercising. I type today's entry with an ice pack pressed against my lower back. I've never enjoyed the pain of working out, but considered it a necessary evil to be a good steward of the body I've been given.

No pain, no gain, right? I guess the jury is still out, except with the Apostle Paul who argued, "Physical training is of little value" (1 Timothy 4:8 — NASB).

As infinite creatures in finite bodies, the temptation is to overly focus on the physical instead of the spiritual. We're all going to die. But not all of us will truly live (John 10:10).

Live each day with your death in mind. Live each day as if it were your last.

Or choose, like so many men, to pour everything into those things that won't pass the test of eternity. The stronger a man is regarding the things of God, the stronger he'll be in Heaven. Heaven, like earth, is a never-ending story of real life, and the pursuit of God.

It's an eternal exploration.

It's going to be awesome!

A man will receive from Heaven what he invests on earth. A man's investment in eternity, while living in the shadow lands, will pay eternal dividends (Matthew 6:19-20).

Live out your short stay on earth with eternity on your mind.

THE AGING MAN

Moses was a hundred and twenty years old when he died, yet his eyes were not weak nor his strength gone.
~Deuteronomy 34:7

In an effort to curtail our imminent mortality and maintain optimal health, the fitness industry has become a multi-billion-dollar-a-year industry. P90X, In sanity, Zumba, and CrossFit are becoming household words in our sedentary world.

They, however, were foreign to our pre-industrial ancestors who stayed fit through good old-fashioned hard work, non-processed foods, and going to bed soon after the sunset.

Moses lived for 120 years and we're told that his strength "never left him" (NASB). Moses reminds me of my Grandpa Ramos who was vigorous up to his dying day at ninety-three years old. One day, at ninety years old, I stopped by to visit and he was on the roof cleaning out the gutters!

All of the men I've known who've aged in the front of the pack had one thing in common. They lived with purpose. Younger men need to follow the example of active, older, godly men who live with purpose.

I knew Grandpa's days were numbered shortly after when he confessed that he picked up leaves in the yard to give him a sense of purpose. He died soon after. His was a life celebrated by many. He was a role model of manhood. Men need something to do. They need a real purpose—a hill to climb and eventually die on.

Men need someone to serve. They need to be something for someone. They need to fight for a cause. A man may retire from his career, but never from serving God. A wise man once said, "May you live all the days of your life."

BLACK AND WHITE

Blessed are they who keep his statutes and seek him with all their heart.
Psalm 119:2

I have a friend who sees the world in black and white. There's no room for gray—only good or bad, right or wrong, black or white.

Life is simple in his black and white world, but every so often his black and white world is shaken by something gray that challenges him to reconsider. The black and white world is simple.

Unfortunately, the black and white world isn't reality.

Life isn't always black and white. For example, to claim alcohol is bad and should never be consumed is a huge leap biblically (John 2:1-10). But to consume alcohol on such a regular basis as to build a tolerance errs on the side of gluttony, drunkenness, and sin.

In the midst of a world that sees gray, what remains black and white? Here it is.

Seeking God with everything we have is black and white for those who claim to follow Jesus. Moderation contradicts the God who said, "Because you are lukewarm—neither hot nor cold—I am about to spit you out of my mouth" (Revelation 3:16).

To view life as black or white, good or bad, right or wrong forces us to choose between two extremes. In life, it can be healthy to live in the gray zone between legalistic and liberal extremes. But with your relationship with God, the world is more black and white than gray.

The God who wants "all your heart" will settle for nothing less. Black.

White.

Gray.

The choice is yours.

TEAM MEETING SEVEN: FRONT END ALIGNMENT

> *"Without the love we had at our first encounter with God, we become seriously out of balance."*
> ~Ken Warner

What did you take away from last week's study and daily readings? What are you still processing? What challenged your current paradigm? What inspired you to grow as a man?

In 2012 the L5/S1 disc in my lower back herniated less that one millimeter back—into the neural canal— causing a condition called Stenosis. That silver-dollar-sized disc resulted in Sciatic nerve pain.

The pain was so severe that a year later I had back surgery. God taught me that, similar to my slipped (herniated) disc, a man is the backbone of his family and must stay in alignment in order for the family to fully function. When a man gets it—everyone wins. When a man is out of alignment everyone loses.

Where have you veered away from the man you claim to be? How have you drifted away from the man you wanted to be in your youth? Have you been thrown out of alignment by an unforeseen bump along the road of life?

By alignment we mean living like the man we claim to be in all facets of life. When the man I claim to be matches the way I live my life—I'm in alignment. In other words, when my public expressions match my private life, I'm in alignment. If, however, my actions don't match my words, I'm a man that's out of alignment.

TEAM MEETING AT A GLANCE

- Opening Prayer, Weekly Announcements
- Personal and Victory Stories
- Each man will share his story — one man per week until all men have shared.
- After all men have shared their personal story, allow time each week for them to share victory stories.
- Weekly Study Closing Prayer
- Closing Prayer

> "Loving devotion to Christ can be lost in the midst of active service."
> ~Alan F. Johnson, *The Expositor's Bible Commentary*

Today we're looking at the Church of Ephesus in Revelation 2:1-5, one of the premier churches of its day, and how it veered off course. We will refer back to this passage throughout the study. Why is it so easy to veer off course spiritually ? How can success cause us to veer off course?

"Ephesus was the greatest city in Asia, claiming as its proud title, 'The first and the greatest metropolis of Asia.' One Roman writer called it the Light of Asia. It was the greatest harbor in Asia; situated by the river Cayster and became a huge trading center making it the wealthiest city in all of Asia. It was the main route from Rome to the East and was one of the few free cities in the Roman Empire, which made it exempt from having Roman troops garrisoned there. It was self-governing as well as being the center of worship for the god Artemis, whose temple was 425 feet long, 220 feet wide and had 120, sixty foot-high columns, and one of the Seven Wonders of the Ancient World."
~William Barclay Commentary

What are the "deeds" listed in Revelation 2:2-4? Can you think of anyone, or church, that fit this description but, over time, veered away from the things of God. What happened to knock them out of alignment? James 1:22-25 and Ephesians 2:10 .

> "In Ephesus, something had gone wrong. The earnest toil was there; the gallant endurance was there; the faultless orthodoxy was there; but the love had gone."
> ~ William Barclay

The propensity of life is to pull us off course. We're eventually pulled into sin when we are out of alignment and it happens easier than you can ever imagine. Imagine a tire of a wheel that has been out of alignment for a long time. You'd quickly notice the wear and tear from being out of alignment.

As men we can get knocked out of alignment when we: 1) hit an unforeseen bump in the road of life, 2) choose a life of secrets and isolation over community, 3) invite the wrong men into our inner circle, 4) pursue the wrong life trophies, 5) get burned out—wounded—by the church, and 6) disengage from those we're called to love and lead.

Like a tire out of alignment over an extended period, a man gets pulled in the wrong direction, wears out sooner than he should, is eventually exposed, is in for a rough ride, and is often replaced before his time.

The Church of Ephesus did all the right things but veered off course (Revelation 2:4). Why must serving God never replace being with God? How can our religious deeds mask a fading faith? What other good deeds could God list in writing a letter to you? (Example: strong in the Word, great servant, generous giver, and passionate evangelist)
Luke 10:38-42

The church in Ephesus would have been the megachurch of its day with the Who's Who of Gentile leaders and wealthy laity. Paul spent more time there than any other of his church plants (Acts 20:31). He even left his spiritual son Timothy as the first pastor over this great church (1 Timothy 1:3) and church tradition hints that Onesimus, slave to Philemon, followed Timothy as pastor some time later. It's Ephesus where we meet Priscilla, Aquila and Apollos. Paul seems to have been closer to this church than any of the others (Acts 20:17-38).

In Revelation 2:4 God says, "But I have this against you, that you have forsaken left your first love." What do you think this love was and why? Why is this the most important thing?
Deuteronomy 6:4-5, Matthew 6:33, 22:37-39, and Philippians 3:12-14.

Westminster Shorter Catechism is a series of questions and answers, written in 1647 with the purpose of educating laypersons in matters of doctrine and belief. It's considered by many Protestants to be the greatest doctrinal statement to come out of the English Reformation. New converts are also given the Westminster Shorter Catechism as well as the Confession of Faith and Holy Scripture to study. Various denominations have used the Westminster Confession and Catechism to instruct their members. The most famous of the questions is:
Q. What is the chief end of man?
A. To glorify God, and to enjoy him forever.

What is often the problem when our relationship with God isn't as strong as it should be? Can you identify any warning signs when a person veers from making Jesus first in their life? Who have you invited to call you out when you get out of alignment?
Deuteronomy 31:6, Matthew 28:20, 2 Timothy 3:16, and Hebrews 13:5

In marriage, the event of falling in love must transition into a lifetime of rising into love for the marriage to thrive. This is what makes strong relationships evolve and grow. The wedding event can't come close to comparing with the marriage process. Marriages struggle when other things take priority over the rising-into-love process. Our relationship with God works the same way. Relationships that work keep first things first. They focus more on the daily process than the random "vacation" events.

What's your greatest challenge in keeping first things first with God? What is your greatest obstacle in pursuing God? Who will lock arms with you in keeping Jesus first?

But I have this against you; that you have abandoned the love you had at first. Remember therefore from where you have fallen; repent, and do the works you did at first. If not, I will come to you and remove your lampstand from its place, unless you repent.
~ Revelation 2:4-5 (ESV)

How do you interpret verse 5 (above)? What three things does God ask the believers in Ephesus to do? How can you personalize this? Do any of these resonate with you?

"In Biblical Hebrew, the idea of repentance is represented by two verbs: shuv (to return) and nacham (to feel sorrow). In the New Testament, the word translated as 'repentance' is the Greek word metanoia, which is a compound word of the preposition meta (after, with), and the verb noeo (to perceive, to think, the result of perceiving or observing). In this compound word, the preposition combines the two meanings of time and change so that the whole compound means: 'to think differently after'. Metanoia is therefore primarily an after-thought, different from the former thought; a change of mind and change of conduct, 'change of mind and heart', or, 'change of consciousness'."
~Wikipedia

Good or bad, remembering events from our past gives life to them. Discuss your early days of walking with Jesus and how they were so inspiring. What was your faith like in those early days when your fire was white hot for God? How has that relationship grown, backslid, or progressed since then?

> *"We lose focus on keeping first things first when we're more concerned about working for God than walking with God."*
> ~Anonymous

> *"Remember where you were. Look at where you are. Remember the white-hot fire you had for God and rise into it again. What did you do when you were on fire for Jesus? Do that!"*
> ~Anonymous

"The imperatives (in Revelation 2:4-5) are instructive: Remember. Repent. Do."
~Expositor's Bible Commentary

What does God mean (vs. 5) when we says, "If you do not repent, I will come to you and remove your lampstand from its place." Is this an idle warning? What would it look like if your lampstand were removed?

"Proof of the ancient Church of Ephesus no longer exists. In fact, there is absolutely no archeological proof of it ever existing. Archeologists found the ruins of the city of Ephesus but no proof of a church. There are fragments of temples and palaces scattered around; but there is nothing to mark the site of a church; there is nothing to indicate even that such a church then existed there."
~Expositor's Bible Commentary

Break into groups of three or four.

Where has your passion to pursue God veered off course?

How can you realign yourself with God?

Take a moment today and pray for each other.

> *"If we love anyone with passionate intensity, we are bound to hate anything that threatens to ruin that person."*
> ~William Barclay

STUDY NOTES

_____
_____
_____
_____
_____
_____
_____
_____
_____
_____
_____
_____
_____
_____

For the next five days, read the following entries from our **The Field Guide: A Bathroom Book for Men.**

We hope they challenge and encourage you to get in the great Arena for God. See you on the Arena Floor!

DESIRE AND LUST

Ants are creatures of little strength, yet they store up their food in the summer.
Proverbs 30:25

Randy showed the pictures of his trophy Mule Deer while recounting each successful hunt. I envied the 6x6 bull, bear, and his many pictures of friends and family with their trophies. He shared story after story and picture after picture.

I was impressed at how a man weighing one hundred pounds less than me could carry a pack equal in weight to mine. Though small in stature, Randy possessed an intense desire that manifested in seemingly enormous strength.

That desire, like the ant, led him to prepare his mind and body beyond what most are willing. Randy taught me that everyone lusts for a great trophy but few have the desire to pursue it.

Lust is impetuous. Desire makes the necessary preparations. Lust is selfish, reckless, and immature. Our world is filled with reactive males who have ruined their lives because of lust, instead of preparing guardrails around their marriages—the way of the man.

Desire prepares. Lust reacts. Men prepare. Males react.

Even the strongest man ill-prepared against lust will fold under minimal pressure. But desire is a game changer. Desire is the catalyst for success in the war over lust. Without it a man will fade to gray. When the going gets tough the "tough" go home with their tail between their legs *if* they haven't made the proper preparations to live a holy life.

Failing to prepare is—you got it—preparing to fail.

Desire for Christ is the key to reaching God's potential. True desire results in realistic preparations and a godly life. Lust unleashed, however, is recklessness, irresponsible, and ill-prepared. Desire has laser focus. Lust is a lantern's light.

Focus your desires on making the proper preparations to guard against lust and maximize your capacity (Hebrews 12:1-2).

CAPACITY

For I am already being poured out like a drink offering...
2 Timothy 4:6

Contrary to what you may think, all men are not created equal. Look around for a second and you'll notice the varying capacities of men. We are finite— limited beings—who God blesses with certain capacities.

The Parable of the Talents in Matthew 25:14-30 is one example of God giving men "each according to his ability." God expects out of you exactly what He has poured into you. The goal of life is to pour out what God pours in.

Strength can be defined as how much you have in your tank. It's your unique capacity. Time is the same for all, but capacities vary according to energy, intelligence, talent, ability, and giftedness.

St. Irenaeus wrote, "The glory of God is man fully alive." A possible interpretation of the "glory of God" is the man who begins each day with a full tank and ends with an empty tank.

It's the man who finishes each day strong.

The goal is to leave it on the field every day—the closer to empty the better. To end each day empty is to steward it for the glory of God. One's capacity compounded daily equals a life. In 2 Timothy 4:6 Paul acknowledges his capacity. Evaluating it, he concludes, "I've been poured out."

His time was complete.

Pour your life into God.

Leave nothing in the tank. Live at full capacity so that one day you may hear: "Well done, good and faithful servant! You have been faithful with a few things; I will put you in charge of many things. Come and share your master's happiness!" (Matthew 25:21)

GOT YOUR BACK

An attacker advances against you, Nineveh. Guard the fortress, watch the road, brace yourselves, marshal all your strength!
Nahum 2:1

In fitness centers, there are often a few guys who purposely neglect working out on important muscle groups, like their legs and back to focus on visible muscles like the chest and arms. There was a time when I avoided my back workouts too. I can't see my back, so why work on what I can't see? I can see my chest, arms, and abs every day.

Yes! Let's pump those up.

But the back, along with the abs, is part of the core. A back injury, unlike other body parts, requires total rest and sometimes surgery. Trust me, I know. Back muscles maintain posture, create an overall sense of balance, and work with the front of our core, the abdominals, to generate power.

Why would anyone ever neglect his back? Strengthen your back and strengthen your core. Who is strengthening your back? A friend once said, "I want guys in my life that have my back."

In other words, he needs men to watch for his blind spots. He needs men who'll sharpen the blade, not stab it into his back. "As iron sharpens iron, so one man sharpens another" (Proverbs 27:17).

Who has your back?

What men have your permission—and the guts—to call you out? What men are helping you navigate by God's truth? What men are exposing the lies in your life? What men have you let into the dark alleys?

Men usually won't watch your back without an invitation. So find a few men today, one or two is a good start, who will watch your back tomorrow.

NORTH TO OREGON

But the Lord stood at my side and gave me strength, so that through me the message might be fully proclaimed and all the Gentiles might hear it. And I was delivered from the lion's mouth.
2 Timothy 4:16-17

Do you have a memory that hurts; a memory so painful that the thought elicits emotion? Such painful memories include the day my parents divorced, the day I found my dog Jesse dead on the side of the road, and the day my favorite grandfather passed away.

But the most painful day was when I moved my wife and sons—ages four, six, and eight—along with everything they knew 1,000 miles north to unknown Oregon. I still get emotional when I remember their expressions of shock, fear, and sadness as they said their final farewells to friends and family, and what would soon be mostly forgotten childhood memories.

Physical pain is easily forgotten. If it weren't, most women would only have one child!

Emotional pain can last a lifetime. Paul's darkest hour was when he stood alone. A tear must have rolled down his weathered face as he recalled, "At my first defense no one supported me, but all deserted me" (2 Timothy 4:16—NASB).

Those closest to him looked the other way. The man who poured his life into others stood alone. Paul had no one to turn to but his God for strength. But how was Paul strengthened?

Was it a five-hour energy drink, a victorious memory, or special insight and wisdom? We may never know. But in Paul's darkest hour, God took his broken spirit and strengthened him. Paul knew what every man should know; that we are never really alone.

If you're reading this as a broken and wounded man, never forget that God stands with you to the bitter end.

LOST MOMENTUM

And what more shall I say? I do not have time to tell about Gideon, Barak, Samson, Jephthah, David, Samuel and the prophets, who through faith conquered kingdoms, administered justice, and gained what was promised; who shut the mouths of lions, quenched the fury of the flames, and escaped the edge of the sword; whose weakness was turned to strength; and who became powerful in battle and routed foreign armies.
Hebrews 11:32-34

Inertia is the state, or quality, in matter that allows it to remain still or motionless. For a moving object, inertia is that thing that keeps it in motion. The way to overcome inertia is by the application of force. Force will cause a motionless object to move. When applied to a moving object force will cause it to slow or stop.

For example, a freight train can be held in a state of inertia with a small brick. At full speed, however, that same train can easily crash through a ten foot, steel-reinforced, cement wall.

Once an object overcomes its state of inertia, its motion creates momentum. The bigger the object in motion is, the greater its potential momentum.

Wow, that's a lot to take in!

So, how does a man, in a state of inertia, who's lost his identity, begin to move forward? How does he gain the momentum needed to propel him through life?

Discovering his masculine identity is the simplest, most radical thing you could ever imagine. By this point in the Field Guide, you may already expect the answer: It's a ruthless commitment to following Jesus with reckless abandon wherever He wants you to go and whenever He wants you to go there.

So, how can a man be like champions in the Bible, whose weakness was turned to strength? Turn your stubborn eyes to heaven. Stop fighting for "a good life" and go all-in for the ride of your life.

TEAM MEETING EIGHT: THE SERIOUS LIFE

> *"I wish I could tell young men that life is more serious than you think. What you do before you turn thirty will affect the rest of your life."*
> ~Ken Warner

What did you take away from last week's study and daily readings? What are you still processing? What challenged your current paradigm? What inspired you to grow as a man?

A friend shared about when he was in college and his godly father confronted him with, "I'm just trying to love you through your stupid years." Similarly, another college-aged man told his father, "This is my time. I want to live my life during my four years of college, then I'll get serious about life."

The problem with this line of reasoning is that the decisions men make from their teen through the college years—good or bad—will carry them through life. Today is dedicated to those wise young men who are trying to get it right the first time. Good hunting.

How were the choices you made in youth more serious than you thought back then? Share an area of sin you experimented with as a young man that you now struggle with as an older adult.

The things I celebrated in my youth, I'm now [ashamed of as a man]. My younger celebrations are my older man distractions.

Let's look to our older guys for the answer to this one. My friend Ken Warner was 75 years old when he inspired the topic of today's meeting, "The Serious Life". What truth do you see in the above statement? What wisdom can we gain from it?

TEAM MEETING AT A GLANCE

- Opening Prayer, Weekly Announcements
- Personal and Victory Stories
- Each man will share his story — one man per week until all men have shared.
- After all men have shared their personal story, allow time each week for them to share victory stories.
- Weekly Study Closing Prayer
- Closing Prayer

> *"The error of youth is to believe that intelligence is a substitute for experience, while the error of age is to believe experience is a substitute for intelligence."*
> ~Ernest Hemingway

Look at Proverbs 27:11-12 (below). How would you use this proverb to admonish a younger man? Where does a young man gain the wisdom needed for life? How do the following verses support the path of wisdom over the foolishness of youth?

Psalm 119:9-16, 71:4-6, Proverbs 5:15-19, 1 Timothy 4:13-14, and 2 Timothy 2:21-23

> *Be wise, my son, and bring joy to my heart; then I can answer anyone who treats me with contempt. The prudent see danger and take refuge, but the simple keep going and suffer for it.*
> Proverbs 27:11-12

What great wisdom did you gain as a young man? Who did you receive it from? What is the tension between gaining wisdom and gaining experience?

What is the dilemma of making wrong choices in youth? How can wrongs choices affect the rest of life? At what point does experimenting with sin become bondage to it?
Job 36:13-15, Psalm 25:6-8, and Ecclesiastes 11:9-10

> *"Moderation creeps up to the line. Self-control stands as far away as possible."*
> ~Anonymous

What are some other ways you can be an example of biblical manhood? Why is it so important to have an intergenerational focus with modeling our faith?
Thessalonians 1:6-8, 2 Thessalonians 3:6-12, 1 Timothy 4:11-16, and Titus 2:6-8

Do not be deceived: God cannot be mocked. A man reaps what he sows. Whoever sows to please their flesh, from the flesh will reap destruction; whoever sows to please the Spirit, from the Spirit will reap eternal life.
Galatians 6:7-8 (NIV)

Life is more serious than you think. One blind spot of young men is their failure to recognize the long-term consequences of sin—which can lead to bondage. What do the following verses teach us about living wisely?
1 Corinthians 6:12-13, 10:11-13, and 1 Peter 2:15-17

When something (or someone) masters us we are no longer free to reject it. We lose the capacity to say, "No!" We lose our freedom and become slaves and addicts.

There are two sides of freedom: self-control and self-discipline. Self-control is the proving ground for freedom. It's the ability to reject—to say, "No." Self-discipline, on the other hand is the ability to say, "Yes" to daily investments in our freedom. For example, to live a healthy lifestyle you must say,

"Yes" to eating right and exercise. Negatively, you must have the self-control to reject processed foods and the sedentary lifestyle.

Freedom is part of God's plan. What does the Bible teach about freedom?
Luke 4:17-19, John 8:31-38, Romans 8:20-21, and Galatians 5:1

"(Freedom is) the power or right to act, speak, or think as one wants without hindrance or restraint."
~ Merriam-Webster, Simple Definition of Freedom

Where does a man draw the proverbial line in the sand in his stance for freedom? How do we remove all stumbling blocks from others and their fight for freedom? Let's use alcohol as an example. What is a good rule of thumb as free servants of God?
Romans 14:13, 1 Corinthians 10:28-30, 2 Corinthians 6:3, Galatians 5:13, and 6:1-2.

If you have any tolerance to alcohol as a believer in Jesus, you may have a problem. If someone you love warns you about your alcohol consumption you probably have a problem. If the law tells you that you have a problem with alcohol you definitely have a problem.

> *"Freedom is a chance to be better."*
> ~Albert Camus

It's true. Life is more serious than we think especially considering our responsibility as free men in Jesus. What is the responsibility given to freed men? How should we be careful in our expression of freedom?

Where have you been overly indulgent in your freedom?

Break into groups of three or four.

Where do you need to start taking your freedom choices more seriously?

Take a moment today and pray for each other.

> *"Liberty means responsibility. That is why most men dread it."*
> ~Franklin D. Roosevelt

STUDY NOTES

For the next five days, read the following entries from our **The Field Guide: A Bathroom Book for Men.**

We hope they challenge and encourage you to get in the great Arena for God. See you on the Arena Floor!

PREVENT DEFENSE

When we heard of it, our hearts melted and everyone's courage failed because of you, for the Lord your God is God in heaven above and on the earth below.
Joshua 2:11

I've never understood why football coaches use a Prevent defense in the final moments of a game. Can someone please help me understand this? For those who don't know, the Prevent defense adds more defensive backs and takes away pass rushers in order to have more guys in coverage.

It's a strategic move away from a game plan in order to prevent defeat. In my experience, all that Prevent does is prevent a team from winning. The bend-but-not-break strategy is soft. The major flaw in Prevent logic is that it hinders the defense from pinning its ears back and doing what got it there in the first place.

It's a try-not-to-lose strategy instead of going big for the win. In today's passage Rahab's (the prostitute) alliance with the spies is motivated by the fear of what God had done so far. She knew the recent history. She saw the smoke. She heard the stories. She saw the storm was coming.

History can be intimidating. All things being equal, a winning program has the upper hand over a losing one based on tradition. Overcoming a history of failure is often the greatest struggle in building a winning life. Memories of failure can create an attitude of caution instead of abandon—a

Prevent defense—that ultimately hinders the pin-your-ears-back pursuit of victory.

Caution is fear of those who are used to losing. But winners hold the trophy before they've won it.

Play to win. Pin your ears back. Go for it.

Face your history. But rewrite your future. Don't play Prevent defense with your life. Forge your future with reckless abandon.

AGAINST THE WIND

Jesus immediately said to them: "Take courage! It is I. Don't be afraid."
Matthew 14:27

As a young boy, our family vacationed north to Nevada's Wild Horse Reservoir. We rented a motor home but our vacation went south as each of us kids got a severe case of the Chicken Pox. The RV had all sorts of problems, and we were thankful to make it home in one piece—barely.

Have you ever had a vacation that fell way short of your expectations? Unfortunately, we live in a world where marriages fail, loved ones get sick, people lose their jobs, and people disappoint us. The storms of life wash away many of our childhood hopes and dreams. The clouds of adversity cover the rays of the sun. Sin crushes the dreams of youth and progress is stalled because "the wind was against us."

Life is more often like the Bob Seger song *Against the Wind*. No matter what we do sometimes, the wind is contrary.

Sometimes we can't do enough to keep the wind from knocking us down. It's in these storms that we are tempted to lose sight of the other side of our dreams. We lose sight of the miraculous power of

Jesus to intervene and calm the storms.

But our Savior has the power to still even the fiercest storm.

Fighting against the wind, the last person the disciples expected to see in the darkness was Jesus walking on water. But there he was! In their face, challenging them to face their fears.

When least expected, there He was coming to their rescue: "Take courage! It is I. Don't be afraid."

SHOT IN THE DARK

O Lord Almighty, God of Israel, you have revealed this to your servant, saying, "I will build a house for you." So your servant has found courage to offer you this prayer.
2 Samuel 7:27

You, my God, have revealed to your servant that you will build a house for him. So your servant has found courage to pray to you.
1 Chronicles 17: 25

I was warned that if I missed the camp from the south, I'd head miles into the canyon and get lost for days. I left camp that morning fully aware to steer north when I came off the mountain.

The Yola Bolly Wilderness is vast and confusing in the pitch black of evening. I'd already missed the surveyor tape I set up to mark my way back as I headed down the wrong ridge. In the midst of my confusion, my headlamp died, and I fumbled in the darkness to find two batteries.

I began to panic: "I'm lost!"

Then I remembered the radio in my pack. I called into the darkness and heard the sounds of laughter and a fire cracking on the other end of the radio. "Fire a shot so we know where you are," I was told. Fifteen minutes later a set of headlights greeted me along with an abusive amount of teasing. I learned that when lost, you have to call out. Sometimes you have to shoot out.

Have you been in a place so dark you couldn't muster the courage to call out to God let alone your wife or friend? In the darkness of sin, sometimes we even lose the desire to pray. The spirit struggles for joy. The heart, swallowed by shadows, forgets to pray.

The key is to turn. Turn from the darkness and find the courage to face the God who's been forsaken. Reach through the darkness and find the light. Call out to Him.

OLD SECOND SHOT

Will your courage endure or your hands be strong in the day I deal with you? I the Lord have spoken, and I will do it.
Ezekiel 22:14

Dad is the king of Buck Fever, earning him the nickname Second Shot. As a youth hunter Dad stressed me out with his excitement in critical situations. It didn't matter how big or small the buck was. Dad showed no prejudice. If it had antlers—Dad lost it.

His mantra being, "You can't boil the horns."

Dad's nerves caused him to punch the trigger instead of pulling it. It's amazing how all bets are off when emotional pressure is heightened. In a 1929 interview entitled "The Artists Reward," Ernest Hemingway defined his usage of the word guts as having "grace under pressure." Ironically, Hemingway took his life in 1961.

In today's passage, God asks Ezekiel a strange question, "Will your courage endure or your hands be strong in the day I deal with you?"

In other words, "How will you handle the pressure when you face me? Will you be able to handle my judgment?"

I've been pretty good over the years of pulling, not punching, the trigger. My secret? I prepare my nerves for high-pressure moments ahead of time so that when they come I'm ready.

Commit to living each day, to the best of your ability. Live each day with abandon. Set the pressure on high in order to have the grace required to pull the trigger when pressured so you don't punch it later.

One day the Creator of the universe will pull the trigger on your life. You will see Him face to face. Will you be ready on that day? Will you have lived everyday like it was your last day?
Can you handle what He will bring your way?

IRRECONCILABLE DIFFERENCES

For everything that was written in the past was written to teach us, so that through endurance and the encouragement of the Scriptures we might have hope.
Romans 15:4

We live in a culture of quitters.

Quitters wear many disguises and have just as many excuses. But the results of quitting look the same; a premature departure from a commitment before that commitment's been completed.

The best aren't necessarily the most talented. A man doesn't have to be the best—he simply has to outlast the rest. This is what it means to finish strong.

A finisher can smell the stench of a quitter from a mile away with his whines and useless excuses. Paul was a finisher. He makes no excuses. He simply writes, "I have fought the good fight, I have finished the race, I have kept the faith" (2 Timothy 4:7).

I have an idea: Make quitting illegal. "Irreconcilable differences" as an excuse for divorce should be a misdemeanor or worse. I bet that would force couples to commit to making their relationship work instead of bailing when the going gets tough.

When raising young men we must help them understand the difference between males and men.

Males start well but finish poorly. Men might start slow, but finish strong.

Success is found on the other side of endurance. The inability to finish is a voided check—useless. It doesn't matter what a man knows if he doesn't have the endurance to finish.

Two things work together to bring us hope, "(through) endurance and the encouragement of the Scriptures we might have hope" (Romans 15:4). Did you catch that? The Bible without an enduring spirit is useless. It doesn't matter how many Bible verses you've memorized if you don't have the endurance to live it out.

"Do not merely listen to the word, and so deceive yourselves. Do what it says," (James 1:22).

TEAM MEETING NINE:
REST: A FOUR-LETTER WORD

> *"Most of the things we need to be most fully alive never come in busyness. They grow in rest."*
> ~Mark Buchanan,
> *The Holy Wild: Trusting in the Character of God*

What did you take away from last week's study and daily readings? What are you still processing? What challenged your current paradigm? What inspired you to grow as a man?

While descending Mt. Whitney in 2000 I ran in to an Irishman who was moving back to Ireland after climbing the mountain. I asked him why he was moving back and I'll never forget his answer—"You".

He said, "Americans are always busy. You work too much."

I agree. Most of the good, hard-working men I know are overworked, over stressed, and under rested. When I compare them (myself included) to Jesus I realize there's a huge canyon between Jesus' pace of life and ours. Jesus was rested, took time for people, and never mentioned how busy he was at work. By our standards, He might be judged as homeless and lazy.

We need a new perspective—a biblical one. We need to give men both permission and the blessing to rest, renew, and reflect weekly without guilt or shame. We need to carve out time for a mental oasis. Rest has become a four-letter word. We celebrate being busy and are ashamed of rest.

Busyness has become a contagious disease. Share your regular Sabbath ritual where, at least once a week, you take time to rest, reflect, and recover. How often do you take at least one day a week to experience a Sabbath rest?

TEAM MEETING AT A GLANCE

- Opening Prayer, Weekly Announcements
- Personal and Victory Stories
- Each man will share his story — one man per week until all men have shared.
- After all men have shared their personal story, allow time each week for them to share victory stories.
- Weekly Study Closing Prayer
- Closing Prayer

> *"I've never heard a dying man say, 'I wish I'd spent more time at the office.'"*
> Lee Iacocca

In his book The Kingdom of God is a Party, Dr. Tony Campolo surveyed fifty, 95-year-olds asking what they would change if they could live life over. Reflecting more on life was one of the top three answers along with risking more and doing more to be remembered for after they had gone.

What is the balance between rest and laziness? Do you tend to work too much or rest too much?
Proverbs 6:6-11, 10:4, 12:27, 2 Thessalonians 3:10-12, and Titus 1:12

What do you think Jesus meant in John 10:10b when he said, "I have come that they may have life (Greek: zoe), and have it to the full." What does the word life mean and how do we experience it for ourselves?

"The Greek word for 'life' is zoe. This is the root of the English words 'zoo' and 'zoology'. Zoe is used of the state of existing and being animate which is common to all mankind, whether saved or unsaved. For example, Paul says to the idol worshipping Greeks at Athens, 'The God who made the world and all things in it...He Himself gives to all life (zoe) and breath and all things...for in "Him we live (zao-the verb form) and move and have our being" (Acts 17:25-28 NASV).

In the Greek New Testament, zoe has a special meaning. It speaks of the life that is given by God through Christ Jesus to those who believe the gospel. In this usage, zoe is often modified by the adjective aionios (English: eon), which means 'eternal', 'everlasting', 'of endless duration.'"
Total Life Ministries

> *"It's essential we prioritize our own physical, psychological, and spiritual vitality, and we can do that in many interactive and productive ways."*
> ~Marshall Shelley

As men of God our life should be different than those around us. How should a Christian man's full life—zoe—differ from the busy lives we're often so tempted by? This may push on our Western mindset, but how should our pace, outlook, and rest be different?

"God is not interested in human beings becoming more refined and cultivated by themselves, in their own life and by their own effort. What He wants is for His zoe life to increase in us, and for us to live by His zoe life and to live out His zoe life. Then the riches of His divine life will be lived out of us, and He will be manifest in our living to the people around us."
~ BiblesforAmerica.org

The word "Sabbath" is mentioned 151 times in the Bible. What is the Sabbath? Why is Sabbath so important to living a full life?
Genesis 2:1-3, Exodus 20:8-11, 31:14-16, Leviticus 23:2-4, Deuteronomy 5:11-15, Matthew 12:1-8, and Hebrews 4:8-10

Charles R. Swindoll said, "God presents the Sabbath rest as a shelter we can enter." What is God's rest? How is it different than simply taking one day off a week?
Hebrews 3:10-12, 17-19, 4:1-4, and 9-11

One Sabbath Jesus was going through the grainfields, and as his disciples walked along, they began to pick some heads of grain. The Pharisees said to him, "Look, why are they doing what is unlawful on the Sabbath?" He answered, "Have you never read what David did when he and his companions were hungry and in need? In the days of Abiathar the high priest, he entered the house of God and ate the consecrated bread, which is lawful only for priests to eat. And he also gave some to his companions." Then he said to them, "The Sabbath was made for man, not man for the Sabbath. So the Son of Man is Lord even of the Sabbath."
Mark 2:23-28

What did Jesus mean in Mark 2:27-28 (above)? God rested on the seventh day but not out of necessity. God created us to sleep one-third of our lives and rest one full day a week throughout our lives. Did you catch that?

> *"On the Sabbath day, we are remembering that my relationship with God did not begin with what I've done, it is not sustained by what I what I do, and it is not guaranteed to the end by my effort or work. I'm saved from beginning to end by Jesus' work."*
> ~Mark Driscoll

Our flesh wants to pursue wealth, power, and success—and it's killing us. If we sow busyness, and unrest in life, we'll reap weak marriages, disconnected children, shallow relationships, and poor physical health. Our failure to sleep and rest is little more than our lack of trust in Jesus to meet our needs. Unrest is trusting in myself more than trusting in Jesus, which is a Christianized version of secular humanism.

Galatians 6:7-9 warns that we will reap what we sow. It's a warning against living to please the flesh. How do you use rest to prevent physical, emotional, and spiritual weariness? How is your busy life working for you? (Defer to the elder statesmen on your team for their experiential wisdom.)

How do you recover on a daily basis? Weekly? What activities fill your tank?

"However, there's a better solution, recovery. The Bible says we should 'not be weary in well doing' (Galatians 6:9). But that does not mean we should become work drudges. We are invited to serve with energy and joy, and that means a rhythm of hard work, yes, but also laughter of friends and the recharging from solitude, and, most of all, the empowering of consistently being true to our deepest values and commitments."
~Marshall Shelley

What are some ways you rest to renew your whole being? Is the busy life really worth the price you'll pay for it? Discuss ways to repent of your destructive habit of unrest.
With tears in his eyes and head hung low a godly Christian man in his sixties shared, "I've worked hard all my life—too hard. I don't remember anything about my children's lives before they were eight years old."

Break into groups of three or four.

Are you taking at least one day off a week to rest and renew yourself?

Are you being obedient to taking a Sabbath?

Take a moment today and pray for each other.

STUDY NOTES

_____
_____
_____
_____
_____
_____
_____
_____
_____
_____
_____
_____
_____
_____

For the next five days, read the following entries from our **The Field Guide: A Bathroom Book for Men.**

We hope they challenge and encourage you to get in the great Arena for God. See you on the Arena Floor!

IF

Here is a trustworthy saying: If we died with him, we will also live with him; If we endure, we will also reign with him. If we disown him, he will also disown us; if we are faithless, he will remain faithful, for he cannot disown himself.
2 Timothy 2:11-13

America held its breath in anticipation as Super Bowl Forty-Two (XLII) entered the fourth quarter. Could the perfect New England Patriots (18-0) defeat the New York Giants to become the greatest team in NFL history?

The 1974 Dolphins went 17-0 and the 1985 Chicago Bears dominated the National Football League going 18-1 on their way to a Super Bowl championship. With barely a minute left, the 2007 New York Giants marched down the field to defeat the Patriots' hopes of a perfect season. What led to their demise?

Were they tired?

Were they cocky? Maybe they failed to see the "end" in "endurance." What caused (arguably) the greatest team in NFL history to end without finishing strong?

If only Eli Manning was injured. If only they didn't complete those clutch passes at the end.

If. If. If. But we'll never know for sure.

The word *if* is mentioned four times in 2 Timothy 2:11-13. Four times. If is the biggest word in the dictionary for only two letters. If is despised by quitters, ignored by champions, and hated by those who end, but don't endure.

Jesus could have whimpered from the cross, "It is over." Instead, He screamed, "It is finished!" (John 19:30).

Live well, finish strong, and leave no room for if.

WEAKNESS EXPOSED

And we pray...being strengthened with all power according to his glorious might so that you may have great endurance and patience.
Colossians 1:10-11

Every January, a new crowd shows up at the local gym with their New Year's resolutions to lose weight and get into shape.

Statistics vary, but in a 2002 study from the University of Scranton, psychologists tracked, for six months, one hundred fifty-nine people who'd made New Year's resolutions. They found that thirty-six percent of resolvers fell off the wagon in the first four weeks.

This survey confirms my observation that by mid-January the gym returns to normal. It takes power to form a new habit.

It takes power to endure.

Quitting exposes our lack of power. To finish with "great endurance" then, is a result of being "strengthened (by God) with all power"."

That being said, let me confess that following Jesus is the most difficult thing I've ever done. It's easy to hide behind grace, allowing my line to go slack and drifting into the waters of sin. But I experience "all power" when I tighten my connection to God through trust.

The problem with power is its propensity to diminish.

How does a man "renew his strength" (Isaiah 40:31) once it's been depleted? Major League pitchers need relief. Cars need gasoline. Guns need ammunition. Workers need vacations. Faith needs rest. A spiritual charge doesn't last forever.

Take a weekly Sabbath.

Rest.

Plug in to the Source.

Recharge and renew.

HEDGING BETS

If we are distressed, it is for your comfort and salvation; if we are comforted, it is for your comfort, which produces in you patient endurance of the same sufferings we suffer.
2 Corinthians 1:6

I was positive that when God asked me to leave my job, become a full time missionary for men, and launch The Great Hunt for God, that it would be a quick and easy death. We had no way to hide it and no way to hedge our bets. We would fail miserably and my only hope was for it to happen quickly. Sink or swim, the world was about to see it. All our chips were on table. We were all in. To our amazement God had other plans.

Bargaining on our part might've been the wise thing to do. Hedging our bets would've been easy. An easy way out usually isn't too hard to find. Listen to the excuses of men hedging their bets:

"If she cheats, I'm gone."

"If I don't like my job, I'll quit."

"If my coach is a jerk, I'm done."

"If I don't like the pastor, I'm leaving."

"If" is the word the quitter uses to bargain away his life. The finisher, instead, adds the word "even" to their "if."

"Even if she cheats, I'll try to work it out."

"Even if I hate my job, I'll work my hardest."

"Even if my coach is a jerk, I'll be a team player."

"Even if the pastor disappoints me, I'll give."

"Even if everyone else quits, I'll be a part of the remnant standing." It's not easy to be all in for God. It's the toughest thing you'll ever do. It's tough because the only way to be all in is to die to yourself and live for Christ. It takes looking beyond yourself.

FROSTBITE

Now you followed my teaching, conduct, purpose, faith, patience, love, perseverance, persecutions, and sufferings, such as happened to me at Antioch, at Iconium and at Lystra; what persecutions I endured, and out of them all the Lord rescued me! Indeed, all who desire to live godly in Christ Jesus will be persecuted.
2 Timothy 3:10-12 (NASB)

I own one pair of boots for hot weather and another for cold. On a recent cold weather hunt, I chose the un-insulated boots and paid the price. We got caught in a snowstorm, leaving two of my toes temporarily numb with frostbite.

If I'd only planned ahead for what was to come. That experience taught me an important lesson in my pursuit of God.

We all experience storms in life.

Whether we're prepared or caught unexpectedly—when then storm hits, the outcome must be the same. We must persevere. In the mountains, and in life, perseverance is the only option other than death. The ability to see the end in endurance forges us through perseverance into the men God desires. Storms are catalysts in developing perseverance.

James 1:2 tells us, "Consider it pure joy, my brothers, whenever you face trials of many kinds, because you know that the testing of your faith develops perseverance." Perseverance requires resistance to pain. Do you want to live for Christ and develop the character trait of perseverance? Good, because the storm is coming. Get ready to experience the "end" of endurance through life's storms. When God forges the character trait of perseverance, He brings severe weather.
Wear your cold weather gear because a storm is brewing!

GIVING UP THE SIDE

He springs up like a flower and withers away; like a fleeting shadow, he does not endure.
Job 14:2

There's a picture on my office with friend Calvin and myself holding and a nineteen-pound Steelhead caught on my first Oregon river trip. As we prepared to drift the Siletz River, our guide warned, "Jim, these are experienced fishermen. Don't be discouraged when they catch more fish."

Fortune was on my side and by the end of the day, four out of six fish boated were on the end of my line, including the monster hatchery hen pictured in my office.

The battle was epic.

I fought her from shore, but twice during the battle we had to get back in the boat, go upstream and get her off boulder snags. I fought her in the rapids for over thirty minutes before she conceded to the pressure of my rod, turned over, and rolled onto her side.

The fight is over when a fish gives up its side.

We aren't so different are we? We fight through the rapids of success and notoriety until the day we realize we don't have much fight left. Secure, we roll over and drift. We give up our side, retire, and float downstream until death takes us home—sometimes drifting aimlessly for over three decades!

The problem: this is not how God made men. Men are not created to drift, float, or give up their side. They're made to fight. But they must fight for the right things. In the end, however, every man surrenders his side to death and is pulled into eternity. Earthly status is washed down the currents of time and all a man has left is what he accomplished for the Master.

Maybe we should consider a cause worthy enough to give our lives to. What are you giving your side to? Have you lost the fight and are adrift, or is there still fight left in you?

TEAM MEETING TEN: FIGHTING SPIRIT

> *"We shall neither fail nor falter; we shall not weaken or tire... give us the tools and we will finish the job."*
> ~Winston Churchill

What did you take away from last week's study and daily readings? What are you still processing? What challenged your current paradigm? What inspired you to grow as a man?

We hope this series of books has been transformative in your journey up and down the mountain of manhood. If you've been blessed by these studies please share your story with us. We love to celebrate victory stories with others. We are easy to reach through our website at meninthearena.com.

We don't believe that men grow the most when they learn but when they teach. Find some friends and start a team of your own, Walk those men through The Strong Men Series.

Send us your team pic so we can celebrate with you. Carefully follow the New Team Launch Steps listed in the back of this book and check out our myriad of leadership resources at meninthearena.org.

Thank you for partnering with us!

> *"A man can travel 7,000 miles around the world, but it's the last thirty inches that really matter."*
> ~Don Owens

TEAM MEETING AT A GLANCE

- Opening Prayer, Weekly Announcements
- Personal and Victory Stories
- Each man will share his story — one man per week until all men have shared.
- After all men have shared their personal story, allow time each week for them to share victory stories.
- Weekly Study Closing Prayer
- Closing Prayer

"Achievement seems to be connected with action. Successful men keep moving. They make mistakes, but they don't quit."
~Conrad Hilton

When you hear the words "fighting spirit" what comes to mind? Why is the fighting spirit so critical to finishing strong? Who in your life models or modeled a fighting spirit?

Today's meeting is dedicated to the memory of my namesake, my Grandpa James "Jimmy" Ramos I. He was the toughest man I've ever known. He lived to ninety-three years old and at ninety he regularly flexed his construction worker forearms and said, "Feel those arms. Pretty solid for a ninety-year-old man, eh?"

He epitomized the fighting spirit until the day he died. Today we're investigating the fighting spirit of Caleb in the Old Testament. At eighty-five years old Caleb is remembered for his words to Joshua in Joshua 14:10-12 below.

How does a man maintain his fighting spirit well into is eighties?

"Now then, just as the Lord promised, he has kept me alive for forty-five years since the time he said this to Moses, while Israel moved about in the wilderness. So here I am today, eighty-five years old! I am still as strong today as the day Moses sent me out; I'm just as vigorous to go out to battle now as I was then. Now give me this hill country that the Lord promised me that day. You yourself heard then that the Anakites were there and their cities were large and fortified, but, the Lord helping me, I will drive them out just as he said."
Joshua 14:10-12

> *"Do not plan for ventures before finishing what's at hand."*
> ~Euripides

Why do men lose their fighting spirit? What is it about life that robs us of our desire to fight? What preparations should we make in the younger years to carry us through the golden years?

The name Mickey Thompson used to be one of the most recognized names in auto racing. His team could build the fastest cars on the track. They could fly! It's interesting, though, that not one of those cars ever brought Thompson the checkered flag. His cars took the lead in the first twenty-nine races they entered, but they never won a race. They never finished! Thompson could build the fastest cars, but not cars that would last. Engines blew. Gearboxes broke. Carburetors failed. The cars began as good starters and quick runners, but were not good for the distance.

In Meeting 8 we learned that life is more serious than we think. It's also more strategic than we think. We can't tell what will happen in life but we can mentally play life's movie and live strategically with the finish in mind. What are you doing now to make preparations for your golden years? (Example: health, retirement, medical, or life insurance.)

Plan for tomorrow today. Invest in your fighting spirit today so that it won't fade away tomorrow.
Take turns reading the section titled "Exploring Canaan" in Numbers 13:1-25. Who can explain what's going on?

Now, silently read the section "Report on the Exploration" in Numbers 13:25-33—specifically Caleb's response (below). What's going on in this passage? How old is Caleb at the time (Hint: Numbers 14:10)? What insights can you gain about Caleb?

> *Then Caleb silenced the people before Moses and said,*
> *"We should go up and take possession of the land,*
> *for we can certainly do it."*
> Numbers 13:40

> *"It's hard to beat a person who never gives up."*
> ~Babe Ruth

In Numbers 14:1-10 the people rebelled against God, and Caleb and Joshua respond by tearing their clothes (14:5-7). Tearing the clothes was generally associated with mourning, and was an expression of deep sorrow and heartfelt grief. It was also a natural reaction at times of great distress and in cases of sincere repentance. Who else was watching his exhibition and how did they react (14:10)? Why do you think Caleb and Joshua did this? What does this say about their spirit?

Because of their disobedience, God prohibited all but Joshua and Caleb from entering the Promised Land. What "different spirit" (14:20-24) did they possess that set them apart in God's eyes? Is it blind chance or random luck that sets some men apart from others? Or have they developed a different—fighting—spirit?
Numbers 14:24, 38, 26:64-65, and 32:11-13

How does radical devotion (see also: Deuteronomy 1:35-36) to Jesus Christ help craft a man's fighting spirit? How does having this spirit help a man to finish strong?
Joshua 14:7-9, Ephesians 6:7-8, and Colossians 3:23

A man's spirit is transformed into a fighting spirit when his spirit is wholeheartedly committed to God's Spirit. Read the below quote from A Chosen Generation founder, Chuck Stecker. What lies have seniors bought into that have robbed them of their fighting spirit? What lies have you bought into about the aging process and your effectiveness for God?

"Our churches have fallen into the unfortunate situation of losing far too many of our seniors who have a significant amount of time and experience to offer to younger generations. This is happening because we have fallen prey to someone wrongfully telling seniors to pass the baton. Do not tell me to pass the baton unless the message you want to relay is that I no longer have any value. If you have bought into the lie and passed the baton, take it back. God will tell you when you are done."
~Chuck Stecker

A few weeks ago, we read a quote that says, "If a man does not finish each day strong he ends it weak, but he must finish more days strong than weak. Weak days compounded equal a weak life." What truth is there in the belief that our life will only be as strong as our daily finishes, compounded over a lifetime?

Break into groups of three or four.

What's one habit you've formed to nurture your fighting spirit?

What baton do you need to take back?

Take a moment today and pray for each other.

STUDY NOTES

For the next five days, read the following entries from our **The Field Guide: A Bathroom Book for Men.**

We hope they challenge and encourage you to get in the great Arena for God. See you on the Arena Floor!

NAME AND NUMBER

But man, despite his riches, does not endure; he is like the beasts that perish.
Psalm 49:12

I have every set of antlers from deer and elk I've taken dating back to 1976. The size of the rack doesn't matter. I keep them all. They're my way to honor a life ended at my hand. Each is named and numbered to recall the story behind the rack.

Who else will remember these animals if not the one who harvested them? As crazy as it sounds there's an overwhelming sense of obligation to honor every trophy even though Psalm 49:12 says, "But man in his pomp will not endure; he is like the beasts that perish" (NASB).

Consider this morbid thought: One day our bodies will be buried in a decorative box (or vase), and either dumped in a hole or burned and spread over the earth. Some will have a headstone with a brief epitaph describing their life. Our body will die. But our soul will endure in the place of your choosing —Heaven or Hell.

What remains of you after you die? What memory will you leave behind? Who will come after you? Who will be better because of you? American Poet, Henry Wadsworth Longfellow (1807-1882) wrote, "Lives of great men all remind us we can make our lives sublime and, departing, leave behind footprints in the sands of time."

Unlike named and numbered antlers, a man's life endures through footprints left in the sands of time. In other words, his memory is in the legacy he leaves in the lives he's impacted. Life is too short to be anonymous and ultimately forgotten soon after death. Plan today for the legacy you'll leave tomorrow.

SCARS

As you know, we consider blessed those who have persevered. You have heard of Job's perseverance and have seen what the Lord finally brought about. The Lord is full of compassion and mercy.
James 5:11

Guys like to tell scar stories. I was with a group of men in Colorado who had a "Scar-Off" at the breakfast table. It wasn't planned but, with men, telling war stories happens naturally. I listened silently waiting for my opportunity until one guy pointed to his forehead, "See this scar? This was where the doctors removed my face."

We put our heads down in defeat and silently went back to eating breakfast. It was male bonding at its finest.

Every scar tells a story about pain. More importantly, however, scars represent healing. The answer to life's pain is found on the other side of the wound. The scar represents a life ready to share its story and lock arms with those suffering from a similar open wound.

Romans 8:28 says, "And we know that for those who love God all things work together for good, for those who are called according to his purpose." Pain, at the time, seems unbearable. Maybe it is. But with God's help—and the help of some scarred friends—you'll get through it. On that day, it'll be your turn to give back. How does God "Work all things to the good?"

He does it by inviting Him into your pain. God wants to walk with you through your pain. He gets it. He experienced pain too. Jesus has scars, "By his wounds we are healed" (Isaiah 53:5).

Scars give us the credibility necessary to bandage open wounds. Maybe your destiny will be discovered among your scars.

Remember, a scar is a reminder of a wound that's been healed.

SEASONS

For everything there is a season, and a time for every matter under heaven....
~ Ecclesiastes 3:1 (ESV)

With a bolt-action .410 shotgun in hand, I walked the railroad tracks at my grandparents ranch in Edna Valley, California, looking for something to shoot. I was nine-years-old and anything dumb enough to come my way was going to get shot at—and probably missed. Whether it was on a telephone wire, in a tree, on the ground, or flying, it was 'go time.' It was my 'Killing Season' as a sportsman and where I learned to love the outdoors.

In the 'Trophy Season' I practiced catch and release, selective water fowling, and searching for the elusive larger antlered game.

As my sons matured and entered the duck blind, I transitioned to the 'Mentor Season,' where others are the beneficiaries of my skills, experience, and opportunities. Success in this season is measured by the success of others— namely, my sons.

A season I have yet to enter is the 'Legacy Season,' where joy is found in the relationships forged. Hunting becomes secondary. True fulfillment is found in nurturing the relationships with trusted friends and loved ones. My dad is in this season.

Each season reflects a man's journey as he moves from learner to legacy leaver. Know the season you're in and your investment for in individuals journeying with you. They're depending on you to point the way. As the Psalmist wrote, "I thought about the former days, the years of long ago" (Psalm 77:5).

As a man matures his influence increases. But, too many men never increase their influence due to immaturity—they remain a male but fail to transition into a man. Joy is found in the legacy created by the relationships nurtured. Success is the ability to pass on the tradition of manhood to your sons and to the men that you mentor.

NAVIGATING

We finish our years with a moan. The length of our days is seventy years—or eighty, if we have the strength; yet their span is but trouble and sorrow, for they quickly pass, and we fly away.
Psalm 90:9-10

Country music star Toby Keith sings, "I ain't as good as I once was, but I'm as good once as I ever was." I've pondered the truth of that song and came to the conclusion that I'm definitely not as good as I once was, and the jury's still out on the latter.

As my sons grow into young men, our wrestling matches are getting more physical, usually ending with my weight overpowering their youth. The longer we wrestle, however, the more winded I become, and the more susceptible I am to their insane onslaughts.

I'm not as good as I once was.

Dad once told me that a man is at his strongest when he's forty. In some ways yes, but forty also means a slower metabolism, longer recovery time, and less cardiovascular capacity. It means larger clothing sizes, stretching my bad back constantly, and shaving my bald head daily.

What does it mean for you?

I'm not as good as I once was.

But I'll never surrender my life to "finish our years with a moan," but with a victory shout. So how do we age with grace? How do we finish the last half of life better than the first? In a word—it's wisdom.

To finish better than you start takes wisdom. It means mentoring younger men who will carry your legacy.

It means never traveling alone. The second half must be spent pouring wisdom and experience into the generations below.

It's about an army of younger men shouting with us instead of a solitary moan.

FINISHING TODAY STRONG

What are those feeble Jews doing? Will they restore their wall? Will they offer sacrifices? Will they finish in a day? Can they bring the stones back to life from those heaps of rubble - burned as they are?
Nehemiah 4:2

Finishing strong is the fifth and final characteristic in The Great Hunt's definition of manhood.

December is the anniversary of my stepfather's tragic death. He was a good man. We had a good relationship. He was respected in his community, worked hard, and had a good life. But sadly his life finished wrong, not strong.

Finishing strong is becoming a lost art among men who give up on marriages, are transient with careers, and believe the lie that retirement is synonymous with finishing.

Completion is not finishing either. Staying in a horrible marriage without fighting to make it thrive is not finishing strong. It's a passive form of quitting. Being alive is not the same as living. The goal of a man is not making it to the end but finishing that end, whenever it may come, as strong as possible.

In Nehemiah we see the Jewish adversaries mocking the construction in Jerusalem. Condescending, Sanballat asks, "Will they finish in a day?" He asked a great question.

The answer is, "Yes."

Do you want to know the secret to finishing life strong? It's finish this day strong. It's that simple. Finishing life strong is the end result of finishing each day strong. Strong finishes compounded over time equal a strong life.

What does that look like? It looks like engaging with your wife and children after work, instead of the television, couch, or a six-pack of beer. It means running hard today, every day, until you lay your head to rest each night. It means reading your epitaph each day you live.

NOW WHAT?!?

You just finished Book 1 of the Strong Men Study Series, defining the five essentials of manhood. You may be wondering, "Now what do I do?"

Thanks for asking. You have three options.
Option Uno: You can look for other resources for the men on your team.

Nah, we're just kidding. That's not an option.
Option Dos: You can move on to one of the other five books in the Strong Men Study Series until you've completed all five books, fifty of the team meetings, and 250 daily readings.

Those books are:

Book 1: The Trailhead: Protecting Integrity

Book 2: The Climb: Fighting Apathy

Book 3: The Summit: Pursuing God Passionately

Book 4: The Descent: Leading Courageously

Book 5: Trail's End: Finishing Strong

Option Tres: Visit our website (www.meninthearena.org) for other great resources to guide you to your best version of a man.

THE BATHROOM BOOK

Men are confused about what a man is. Is he a hunter, an extreme sports guy, or religious? Is he strong, a warrior, or a fighter? Is he a great athlete, rich, or famous?

Better yet, how does a male know when he's crossed into manhood? Is it chronological age? Is it anatomical? Is it when he is legally called a man? Is it becoming financially independent?

Where does a man learn about being a man? Is it from his dad, a coach, television, Google, The Bachelor, or possibly Chuck Norris?

In the Field Guide: A Bathroom Book for Men, Jim Ramos uses his unique storytelling ability to tie masculine words in Scripture with everyday life. Day after inspiring day, the Field Guide weaves biblical themes of masculinity throughout the five essentials of manhood, "protecting integrity, fighting apathy, pursuing God passionately, leading courageously and finishing strong."

This book is a must-read for men. Place it at your bedside, in your office, man cave, or the back of your toilet. Use it as your favorite bathroom book. Read it daily. But be careful. The paper is no substitute for the real deal and will cut you! Only use it for reading!

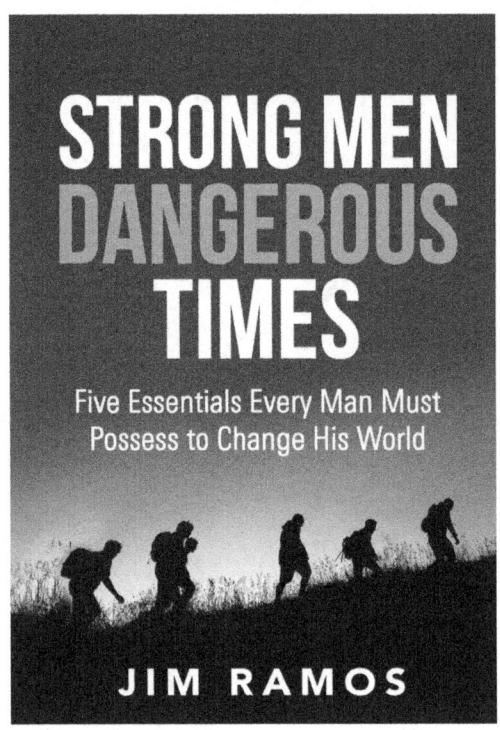

STRONG MEN DANGEROUS TIMES

Weldon M. Hardenbrook wrote, "Let's face it. It's extremely difficult for men to act like men when so much confusion exists about the definition of manhood. For most of human history, people knew what it meant to be a man. Now, at least in modern America, no one seems to know."

But men are conquerors. They seek the next hill to die on. They long for a mission to accomplish. They need a target to shoot at, but the sights have become blurry. Men are staring aimlessly through a dense fog of cultural ambiguity, and those they love are paying the price.

In his book Strong Men Dangerous Times: Five Essentials Every Man Must Possess to Change His World, Jim Ramos answers the question men have been asking for years, "What is a man?"

The simplicity of the book is brilliantly designed for the man who's too busy to read. It's short, to the point, and loaded with life application stories and will keep you on the edge of your seat!

Order your copy today.

ENLIST IN OUR ARMY

Facebook Forum
Join thousands of men from around the world in an open discussion on manhood! The Men in the Arena is a closed group for men only. It is the best free resource for men to discuss what a man is and does. Get out of the anonymous bleachers and into the Arena today!

Weekly Equipping Blast
Visit our website and subscribe to our weekly Equipping Blast. This is not spam or advertising. It is our weekly effort to guide you towards your best version.

Podcast
Subscribe to the Men in the Arena Podcast and learn from the top authors and experts on manhood on the planet.

GLOSSARY

The Definition (aka Five Essentials or Man Card): The Men in the Arena definition of manhood is "protecting integrity, fighting apathy, pursuing God passionately, leading courageously, and finishing strong." These are the things a man does to keep his Man Card.

Dioko: The Greek word the Apostle Paul used in Philippians 3:12 and 14 for "press on" meaning to hunt, pursue, or chase. It's where our name for The Great Hunt for God originated before we changed it to Men in the Arena!

Equipping Blast: Our weekly email blast is sent to thousands of men around the world. It includes our blog, podcast links, training videos, and more! Sign up at meninthearena.org.

Fighting Apathy: The second of the five characteristics of manhood demanding that men fight against all cultural resistance threatening to pull them down. Failure to resist this friction over time becomes apathy or callousness. Matthew 13:13-15 defines "callousness" as a lack of feeling that results when we fail to fight against the things trying to push us down. The second book in the Strong Men Study Series: The Climb, is dedicated to this topic.

Financial Champion: Did you know Men in the Arena is a crowd-funded organization? Crowd-funded means we strategically partner with generous people like you to fund our ministry. Please consider joining our great team of financial champions by signing up as a monthly donor on our website.

Finishing Strong: This is the last of the five traits of manhood, imploring men to finish every day strong to finish life strong. Each day's strong finish compounded over time completes a strong life finish.

Finishing is not the same as finishing strong. Please refer to 2 Timothy 4:6-7. The fifth book in the Strong Men Study Series: The Trail's End is dedicated to this topic.

Guardrails: Imagine traveling on the narrow road Jesus spoke of in Matthew 7:13-14. Its borders are lined with guardrails meant to direct and protect you as you travel through life. Guardrails are walls or hedges a man builds around himself and those he loves. Deuteronomy 22:8 is a great reference for building guardrails.

Intergenerational: One of the core values of the Men in the Arena is to lock shields with men representing all generations and decades of life.

Leading Courageously: The fourth of five aspects of The Definition imploring a man to step up and assume the role as patriarch and spiritual leader of the household. The fourth book in the Strong Men Study Series: The Descent, is dedicated to this topic.

Protecting Integrity: The first and foundational component in the Man Card describing the man who is mature, complete, and unbroken. Integrity is the sum of all character traits fully formed in a man. The first book in the Strong Men Study Series: The Trailhead, is dedicated to this topic.

Pursuing God Passionately: The third and climactic component of the Man Card. It's our adamant belief that no man can achieve his original design without radical obedience and relentless pursuit of his Creator and King. The third book in the Strong Men Study Series: The Summit, is dedicated to this topic.

Tag Line: We say it all the time. "When a man gets it - everyone wins!!"

Team Meeting: The weekly gathering of the Men in the Arena. Team meetings are designed to be no more than one hour in length and set to meet at the same time and place each week at the discretion of the team captains.

Vision: Our vision is simply trusting Jesus Christ to build an army of Men in the Arena, who are becoming their best version in Christ, and changing their world (because when a man gets it - everyone wins!).

COACHING TIPS

This Coaching Tips section is designed to help both new and seasoned Team Captains.

It offers helpful hints we've discovered in our years of running small groups with men.

Our one request is that you don't veer off course and go rogue with your team meetings. Our coaching tips are tried and true.

Feel free to add your personal style but avoid making it up as you go. We've been there—done that— and want to spare you the humiliation! Good hunting.

Big brother is watching: Your guys are watching you. They're watching how you live, love, serve, and run all team meetings.
Be an example.

Bring your A-Game: Bring your A-Game to the team meetings. Know who will and will not be present. Come prepared with notes in your workbook. If you have a co-captain, make sure you're on the same page. Men know when you come unprepared. This sends the wrong message.

Dynamics: How your team members are positioned in the room is crucial. The men need to sit at eye level and equidistant from the center of an eight-foot (maximum) diameter circle. If your circle, or any man, is further than four feet from center, your discussions will be greatly hindered.

Finger on the pulse: Your team will take on a unique identity. The morale of the men is at different levels, and group dynamics change constantly. What is the heartbeat of your men? Who's been missing? Who seems disengaged? Are you connecting with your co-captain(s)? What does your team need this week?

Floor Stare: Try this the next time you ask a question. Stare at the floor or at your workbook until guys begin to answer. Let them deal with the awkward silence and figure out an answer on their own.

Half Full Glass: Transforming lives is a journey. It's an investment into the lives of imperfect men. Even though these books are broken into ten-week bricks, our goal is to make a long-term investment in the transformational process.

But life is tough, and people are messy. When you lead your team, make sure to be positive. The negative will be easier to spot but be careful to acknowledge more positive than negative. It will pay dividends in the end.

Preparation is Key: Come prepared and ready to lead your team each week. The men on your team are watching you. They see the scribbled pages of preparation within the margins of The Man Card Series pages.

They also notice the blank pages when you come unprepared. Don't wing it and fling it. Bring your own thoughts and ideas to the table at every team meeting.

NEW TEAM LAUNCH STEPS

The Launch Steps are a tool to help Captains start a successful team.

Launch Step One: Co-Captain
Although it is not mandatory that you do this to launch a team, we highly recommend that you have another man to lock shields with through this process. There will be times you can't make it to the group, and it's good to know that someone has your back.

Besides recruiting team members, leaders often confess that finding their co-captain was the most challenging step in launching a new team. If you already have your co-captain, great job!

If you're struggling to find a co-captain, don't be discouraged. It's normal! When you approach a potential co-captain, and he has questions about the Men in the Arena and what you're asking him to do, send him to our website (www.meninthearena.org).

There, he can join our online forum, subscribe to our Equipping Blast, and receive all the information about Men in the Arena he needs to feel confident. Now you're ready to take on Launch Step Two.

Launch Step Two: Hit List
Hopefully, you were able to recruit a co-captain. If so, congratulations! Now it's time to put together your team. That's what building the Hit List is all about. Did you know that Jesus recruited a larger group of disciples before he chose the Twelve? Check it out:

"One of those days, Jesus went out to a mountainside to pray, and spent the night praying to God. When morning came, he called his disciples to him and chose twelve of them, whom he also designated apostles: Simon (whom he named Peter), his brother Andrew, James, John, Philip, Bartholomew, Matthew, Thomas, James, son of Alphaeus, Simon who was called the Zealot, Judas, son of James, and Judas Iscariot, who became a traitor."
Luke 6:12-16

With your co-captain, create two Hit Lists of at least 10-15 potential recruits—yours and his. Commit your Hit List to prayer, asking God to direct you through the process.

Once both lists have been compiled, pray over them, and decide who will receive a formal "call" (Launch Step Three) to be on your team. Some Team Captains invite all the men on their Hit Lists, while others are more selective. This is personal preference. Some Captains struggle to recruit enough men for their team. Others have to cut their Hit List down. Team size should range from a minimum of six to fourteen members maximum.

If possible, create an intergenerational team of men ranging throughout multiple decades of life. Once the Hit List is created, move on to Launch Step Three.

Launch Step Three: Call
Before you call each man, make sure you have the set time, date, and place of your first meeting—the Team Launch. This is important: you and your co-captain set the meeting day, time, and place, then tell the men. Don't ask the men what they prefer.

Make a decision before inviting men to join your team. Captains that try to please everyone on this issue lose. Some men won't be able to join your team simply because of your meeting times. That's normal, and you must be okay with it.

Once verbal commitments are made, move on to Launch Step Four.

Launch Step Four: Team List
How Captains communicate with their teams is partly what separates the good teams from the great ones. The Team List will be used on the Buy-In (Launch Step Six) and must include: Name (and wife's name), e-mail (and wife's e-mail), and cell phone number. The sooner an e-mail and text group are created, the more effective your team will be.

Use the Team List to remind the men about your weekly meetings. This acts as a reminder and gives men a simple way to reply if they can't make it that week.

We recommend putting together a calendar of key events for your team. Include your launch day, time, and place of weekly meeting, Team Potluck (Launch Step Five), and other important dates such as birthdays, important anniversaries, and regular social gatherings.

Launch Step Five: Team Potluck

You're almost there! You only have a few more steps until your Team Launch! Great job! We can't overemphasize the importance of the Team Potluck, especially for the married men. Use your Team List to communicate the time, date, and location of the Team Potluck.

Give your potential team at least three weeks' notice to save the date and communicate with their wives (Who should also be included in the email). We have found that the wives are usually the ones who manage the family calendar.

You should also invite the pastor who oversees small groups at your church. Have him pray for the meal and say a few words about the value of men in God's agenda.

Your goal is 100% attendance of those invited. One Team Captain confessed that he opted out of the potluck to hurry the process, and it was a monumental mistake.

The goal of the Team Potluck is to get total buy-in from the wives and have all questions answered. If the wife is in, the man is in. Trust us! We've seen it over and over. Attendance by the wives is critical for the success of Team Potluck.

Team Potluck Sample Agenda
- Dinner Responsibilities
- Captains supply the drinks and dessert
- Host home supplies dinnerware
- A-M Main Dish
- N-Z Salad (or dessert)

Sample Agenda (make it better)
- Fellowship
- Food (remember to pray before eating!)
- Captain and wife introductions
- Team member and wife introductions
- Review Team Launch information (day, time, and place), commitment level (75% attendance), and other pertinent information
- Explain the Buy-In (Launch Step Six)
- Q and A
- Pray for the group

Team Captain Commission: We believe in partnership with the local church and highly encourage Team Captains to get commissioned by a pastor or spiritual leader. If at all possible, get commissioned during the worship service at the church you attend. If not, the potluck is an appropriate option.
Fellowship

Launch Step Six: Buy-In
You can almost taste your Team Launch at his point. We're as excited as you to see lives transformed through your team!

All that's left is to order the books. Attrition will most likely claim some of the men, but we have found that the more the men buy in, the more committed they will be.
You can either buy the resources yourself, and the men reimburse you or send them directly to www.meninthearena.org and purchase the curriculum themselves.

Launch Step Seven: Commission and Launch
We hinted at this in launch Step Five: Team Potluck. Did you know that in the New Testament, the Twelve Apostles, the Apostle Paul—and Jesus—were commissioned in ministry? Have you been commissioned?

If not, we highly recommend it as a model for spiritual leadership. We believe so much in the local church that we strongly urge all team captains to be commissioned by their pastor or spiritual leader. Make it a public display. Here are some elements of a commission.

- Ceremony or public worship service
- Anointing and/or laying on of hands
- Public words of affirmation
- Giving of gifts (optional)
- Witnesses
- Spiritual leader
- Predecessor
- The Holy Spirit

Launch Step Eight: Team Launch Meeting One
Today's the day you've been working so hard for—Congratulations! This is an informational meeting only. Do not plan on going through the curriculum. Rather, make sure all of the men have it. If you don't meet where food and drinks are served, make sure they are available. Your first meeting should be one hour long from your designated start time (start on time, end on time).

Below is a sample agenda.
- Fellowship over food and drinks (10 minutes)
- Opening Prayer
- Restate the purpose, expectations, meeting agenda. Make sure they have purchased their books. (5 minutes)
- Men share about their lives, what they expect to get from the group, and where they are in their spiritual journey (40 minutes)
- Encourage and inspire them with your personal vision for the team. Be sensitive to where each man is. Be careful not to push too hard too fast. (5 minutes)
- Closing Prayer

Thank you so much for getting out of the anonymous bleachers and into the Arena! We are pumped to partner with you on your new adventure!

ABOUT JIM RAMOS

Thank you for taking your precious time to work through this book. I am honored and hope it inspired you on your journey towards the best you.

Lets lock arms on our journey. You can follow my journey on Facebook, Twitter, or Instagram @jimwramos.

I've been married to my best friend Shanna since 1992. She's the most important person in my life and my best friend. We love drinking coffee, traveling to tropical places, and eating out with friends.

I'm an avid book reader, enjoy fitness in the great outdoors, but my real passion is hunting. My sons are my hunting partners, along with a select few guys.

I love hanging out with men over a cup of good coffee and learning their stories. You can learn more about my story at meninthearena.org

Made in the USA
Monee, IL
24 December 2021